# Top 80 Keto Pressure Cooker Recipes

Easy, Healthy, Delicious Ketogenic Diet Recipes Cookbook for Your Electric Pressure Cooker

Ellen Branson

All rights Reserved. No part of this publication or the information in it may be quoted from or reproduced in any form by means such as printing, scanning, photocopying or otherwise without prior written permission of the copyright holder.

Disclaimer and Terms of Use: Effort has been made to ensure that the information in this book is accurate and complete, however, the author and the publisher do not warrant the accuracy of the information, text and graphics contained within the book due to the rapidly changing nature of science, research, known and unknown facts and internet. The Author and the publisher do not hold any responsibility for errors, omissions or contrary interpretation of the subject matter herein. This book is presented solely for motivational and informational purposes only.

# Contents

**Introduction: Why Do You Need This Book?** .................................. 1
**Keto Diet Basics** ................................................................................ 2
    What is the Ketogenic Diet? ............................................................. 2
    Foods to Eat During the Keto Diet .................................................. 2
    Foods to Avoid During the Keto Diet .............................................. 6
    Appliances Used In Cooking Keto Foods ......................................... 7
    Principles for Staying with Keto and Notable Points ...................... 9
    Benefits of Keto Diet - Is it for Everyone? ..................................... 10
**Breakfast Recipes** ............................................................................ 11
    Coconut Porridge ........................................................................... 12
    Chiles Quiche .................................................................................. 13
    Spinach Quiche ............................................................................... 14
    Bacon & Egg Cups .......................................................................... 16
    Veggie Muffins ................................................................................ 17
    Scallion Omelet ............................................................................... 19
    Bacon & Kale Casserole ................................................................. 21
    Sweet Potato Casserole ................................................................... 22
    Veggie Casserole ............................................................................. 24
**Starter & Snack Recipes** ................................................................. 26
    Scotch Eggs ..................................................................................... 27
    Bacon Wrapped Asparagus ............................................................ 29
    Buffalo Chicken Dip ....................................................................... 30
    Boiled Peanuts ................................................................................ 31

Roasted Pecans ............................................................................. 32

**Soup Recipes ............................................................................. 33**

Onion Soup .................................................................................. 34

Pumpkin Soup ............................................................................. 35

Broccoli Soup .............................................................................. 36

Carrot Soup ................................................................................. 38

Cauliflower Soup ......................................................................... 40

Bacon & Veggie Soup .................................................................. 41

Cheeseburger Soup ..................................................................... 42

Chicken Soup .............................................................................. 43

Creamy Chicken Soup ................................................................. 44

Meatballs Soup ............................................................................ 46

**Meat Recipes ............................................................................. 48**

Shredded Chuck Roast ................................................................ 49

Braised Chuck Roast ................................................................... 51

Beef Short Ribs ........................................................................... 53

Beef Curry ................................................................................... 55

Beef with Mushroom Sauce ......................................................... 57

Beef with Broccoli ....................................................................... 59

Beef with Bell Peppers ................................................................ 61

Ground Beef Curry ...................................................................... 62

Meatballs in Gravy ...................................................................... 64

Herbed Meatloaf .......................................................................... 66

BBQ Pork Ribs ............................................................................ 68

Pork Chops .................................................................................. 70

Leg of Lamb ................................................................................ 71

Lamb Shanks ............................................................................... 73

  Lamb Curry .................................................................... 75

**Seafood Recipes** ................................................................ **77**

  Steamed Salmon ............................................................ 78

  Feta Salmon .................................................................. 79

  Cod with Tomatoes ....................................................... 80

  Fish Curry ..................................................................... 82

  Nutrition Information per Serving: ............................... 83

  Shrimp Curry ................................................................ 84

  Creamy Shrimp ............................................................. 86

  Creamy Lobster ............................................................. 88

  Lemony Mussels ............................................................ 90

  Mussels in Tomato Gravy ............................................. 92

  Buttered Crab Legs ....................................................... 93

**Vegetarian Recipes** ........................................................... **94**

  Beet Salad ...................................................................... 95

  Creamy Cauliflower Rice .............................................. 96

  Cheesy Zucchini Noodles ............................................. 97

  Buttered Asparagus ....................................................... 98

  Buttered Brussels Sprout ............................................... 99

  Garlicky Broccoli ......................................................... 100

  Feta Green Beans ........................................................ 101

  Cheesy Cauliflower ..................................................... 102

  Creamy Mushrooms ................................................... 104

  Spinach with Cottage Cheese ..................................... 106

  Spiced Kale .................................................................. 108

  Zucchini with Tomatoes ............................................. 110

  Mixed Greens Curry ................................................... 111

Eggplant Curry ............................................................. 113

　　Mixed Veggies .............................................................. 115

**Poultry Recipes** ................................................................. **117**

　　Roasted Cornish Hens ................................................. 118

　　Roasted Chicken .......................................................... 120

　　Stuffed Chicken Breast ............................................... 122

　　BBQ Chicken Thighs ................................................... 124

　　Chicken Legs ................................................................ 126

　　Butter Chicken ............................................................. 128

　　Chicken Curry .............................................................. 130

　　Cheesy Chicken ............................................................ 132

　　Roasted Duck ............................................................... 134

　　Roasted Quails ............................................................. 136

**Dessert Recipes** ................................................................. **138**

　　Yogurt Custard ............................................................. 139

　　Chocolate Mousse ........................................................ 141

　　Crème Brûlée ............................................................... 143

　　Lemon Cheesecake ....................................................... 145

　　Chocolate Cakes ........................................................... 147

# Introduction: Why Do You Need This Book?

This cookbook contains all the recipes that can be cooked in the pressure cooker and are ketogenic as well. Diet that comprises low carbohydrates, adequate protein, and high amounts of fat is referred to as the ketogenic diet. It is much easier to grab and eat ready-made food rather than cook food all from scratch. Our health has been badly influenced by our busy life schedules. For this reason, people try to find convenient and easier ways to stay healthy and eat healthy. The solution to all these problems is this cookbook, which has all these ketogenic recipes cooked in an Instant Pot. I will discuss the details about the ketogenic diet and the specialty of the Instant Pot in this cookbook.

# Keto Diet Basics

## What is the Ketogenic Diet?

Tthe ketogenic diet plays an essential role in the field of medicine as it is used to treat epilepsy in children. High carb intake leads to the production of glucose and insulin. They compel the body to utilize glucose as a central form of energy, which causes the fats to be stored in the body. In this case, the diet has very little carbohydrate, fat is converted into fatty acids, and ketone bodies by the liver. The ketone bodies serve the function of passing into the brain and substituting glucose as an energy source.

The ketogenic diet plan is an effective way to help you get rid of your obesity. It helps with weight loss, so it's an attraction for all of us. This diet plan wasn't very popular previously, but nowadays, it has gained a lot of importance. The keto diet helps you fight diabetes and epilepsy as well, so it is very important medically. It is rich in fats but low in carbohydrates. When a person starts eating according to the keto diet plan, their body is sent into ketosis. When the body adapts to ketosis, it consumes fats as a source of energy rather than carbohydrates. Dieticians who have got a complete understanding about the keto diet plan tell us about the foods we should eat and those which are to be avoided during the keto diet.

## Foods to Eat During the Keto Diet

There is a list of foods to be eaten when you want to adopt ketosis. The list of foods allowed includes:

### Low-Carb Vegetables

Vegetables are rich in fiber content. Our bodies do not digest these fibers like carbohydrates or calories. They are also rich in vitamins like vitamin C. Non-starchy vegetables provide a lesser amount of calories and carbohydrates but contain a lot of nutrients. Vegetables like potatoes, yams, and beets contain high contents of starch, so they must be avoided during keto diet.

## Seafood

The ketogenic diet plan contains a lot of seafood. Fish, shellfish, and salmon contains vitamins and is good in the keto diet. They are free of carbohydrates but provide potassium and selenium as well. However, some edibles obtained from the sea may contain a greater amount of carbohydrates, so keenly observe your net carb intake.

## Meat and Poultry Items

We do not have to fear that eating meat and poultry items will raise our carb content. They are frequently eaten during the keto diet because they are rich in vitamin B and other minerals like potassium and selenium but contain no carbs. When you eat a low-carb diet, there is a chance that your muscles might be affected. But meat and poultry saves you from the threat, providing you with a high protein content that feeds your muscles.

## Cheese

Cheese favors your keto diet, providing you with a good amount of fats. It provides nutrition and is trendy. For instance, one ounce of Cheddar cheese gives you seven grams of protein and one gram of carbohydrates. Cheese contains a high amount of saturated fatty acids but still does not increase the chance of medical problems like heart disease, and may be protective against them.

## Plain Greek Yogurt and Cottage Cheese

These food items aren't fully free from carbs and contain some amount of carbohydrates but also provide proteins. These are favorable for those who follow the Keto diet plan. These food items increase your appetite and enhance the feeling of fullness, so they are good during the keto diet. Both of these provide five grams of carbs. Greek yogurt provides eleven grams of proteins, whereas cottage cheese provides eighteen grams of it.

## Eggs

Eggs trigger hormones and enhance the feeling of fullness when eaten. The egg we eat contains up to six grams of proteins and less than one gram of carbs. It is frequently eaten almost all over the planet. Because it gives you a feeling of fullness, it helps you avoid eating extra calories. Eating eggs are also good for your sight and contain antioxidants.

## Butter and Cream

These are the food items that contain a low amount of carbohydrates but are rich in fats. These food items are rich in saturated fatty acids. It was believed that they may cause heart diseases, but as the research developed, we came to know that this isn't the only reason for heart problems.

## Dark Chocolate and Cocoa Powder

Cocoa has a great antioxidant action. It is called a super fruit because of its great anti-oxidative function. Flavanols are present in dark chocolate, which are antioxidants. They help maintain the health of arteries, hence help maintain blood pressure. Normal blood pressure prevents heart diseases from occurring. We can add dark chocolate to our keto diet, but it must contain 70 percent cocoa solids.

## Nuts and Seeds

Nuts and seeds are tasty and nutritious. They give you many fats but lesser carbohydrates so are good for your keto diet plan. Nuts and seeds are also a good source of fibers and absorb calories from the body. They have a good medical importance and prevents the occurrence of cancer, heart diseases, and depression. The nuts we eat vary in their amount of carbs. Different nuts that are preferable for your keto diet include: macadamia nuts, walnuts, pecans, pistachios, chia seeds, flax seeds, and sesame seeds.

## Coconut Oil

Coconut oil contains medium-chain triglycerides. The liver processes these and directly converts them into ketone bodies, which can be used as source of energy for the body. Brain diseases might occur due to decreased ketone bodies, and coconut oil is also good for such problems.

## Olives

Olives give you many health benefits. You can eat them during your keto diet plan. The active constituent or main component is oleuropein. It has antioxidant properties and contains many carbs. But most of them are present in fibers so are digested.

## Berries

Berries are fruits that are low in carb content. They contain digestible carbs in the form of fiber. Berries have anti-oxidative properties and protect you from diseases. Black berries, raspberries, and blueberries are examples. Though other fruits aren't allowed to be eaten when you are on the keto diet, berries have a different position.

## Shirataki Noodles

Shirataki noodles are made from glucomannan and are mainly water. They contain six calories and one gram of net carbs in each serving. These fibers are gelatinous and decrease gastric motility. Hence, you feel less hungry. This is effective when you are on a weight-loss plan.

# Foods to Avoid During the Keto Diet

Here we have a list of foods we ought to stay away from when we are following the keto diet plan. The keto diet is a high-fat, low-carb, and moderate-protein diet that you can enjoy.

## Starch

When you are on the keto diet, avoid eating all food items that contain starch. Also avoid whole sugar and its products. When you are on a keto diet, you have to pay attention to your net carb intake. Starch is a carbohydrate actually. So it goes against your desire for weight loss. Avoid:

- Bread
- Pasta
- Rice
- Potatoes
- French fries
- Chips
- Museli
- And Whole Grains like Lentils

Here, one thing that is important to mention is that we have replacements for all of these in the keto diet plan. Replacements are also present for sweeteners that you add to your food items.

## Beer

Beer is strongly prohibited if you are a follower of keto diet plan. There are many dissolved carbs present in beer. The liquid form of carbohydrates isn't what your weight loss plan demands. However, there are some beers with lower carb content.

## Fruits

Fruits are high in carbohydrate content. Fruits are nutritious and delicious but do not fit the requirement of the keto diet plan. There are certain fruits which are allowed to be eaten during ketosis but still the demand is of high-fat and low carbs. So avoid eating fruits.

## Margarine

Margarine is a modified form of butter. It is prepared by industries. A general survey among the people who eat it says that it is bitter in taste. It contains omega-6 fatty acids. Doctors who guide you about your nutrition say that it must be avoided if you are eating a keto diet.

# Appliances Used In Cooking Keto Foods

Every task has its own requirements. If you are planning to work in the kitchen and are about to prepare foods based on keto diet, then you must have following appliances in your kitchen.

## Ingredients Cookbook

If you are following a keto diet plan, then you have to restrict yourself within the boundaries this diet plan offers. When you are working in the kitchen according to the keto diet plan, then you must have this cookbook with you. It is specifically for keto recipes and requires the use of specific appliances. You can easily prepare tasty and trendy food items easily and can also save time.

## Beginner's Guide Cookbook

You need to have this book in your kitchen if your interaction with the keto diet has just begun. It contains easy tricks, tips, and recipes. You will feel at home with the keto diet if you introduce this cookbook to your kitchen.

## All-in-One Food Processor and Blender

Another important electrical appliance that you should keep in your keto kitchen. It is a very helpful device because it easily blends your food and thoroughly processes it.

## Cutting Boards

We often have wooden boards in our kitchen that are used for cutting vegetables or meat. These are also needed when working with the keto diet. You can easily obtain meat and vegetables in acceptable and required sizes by using cutting boards.

## Immersion Hand Blender

This is very helpful if you are making soups. It can also help you prepare healthy sauces and elixirs. No need of cleaning a Vitamix.

## Measuring Cups and Spoons

Certain food ingredients are necessary to be measured, and if they are added without accurate proportion, they may spoil your dish. Your keto kitchen must have these.

## Food Scale

This is an appliance used to measure the food you are cooking. Though it's not always necessary to measure the food you are cooking, doing this may help you get better output.

## Vacuum Sealer

One problem we often face is storing and refrigerating food, especially meat products. Vacuum sealers are very helpful if you want to store and divide meat. You can save meat for a long time by using this device.

## Cast Iron Kit

This is one of the major appliances among your list used in cooking keto foods. It can work like an oven and can even give you foods you prepare using a low flame. It is usually a slow cooker and retains heat. This is very effective in thorough and delicious cooking.

## Spiralizer

You need spiralizer if you want to pull off your low-carb content. This is your basic need in a keto kitchen.

# Principles for Staying with Keto and Notable Points

There are some important points which should be kept in mind. Actually, these are certain trends to be adopted while living according to the keto diet. It is important to have a complete know-how about GP whenever you start a diet plan. It's important to know the condition of a person before he or she starts treating himself in a different way or something different from routine. Precautionary measures are present in every case that might be pregnancy or a diseased person. Age factors must be considered as well because elderly patients might show a negative response to the new routine.

When the body starts ketosis, it uses fats as fuel instead of carbohydrates. Carbohydrates are preserved inside your body, so keenly observe your net carb intake. The ketogenic diet boosts your body for insulin production. It is medically helpful.

Previously we had a different version of the keto diet. When a person ate that diet, they became victim to nutritional deficiencies. Eventually, weakness occurred and the person felt dizzy. There were also health issues possible. While eating the old version of the keto diet, a person could lose focus as well. But now, we use an updated version of keto diet which is mostly free from such problems.

The new version is more fruitful because it allows you to eat foods that contain proteins. Proteins provide you with health and energy. But it does not allow you to increase carb intake. Whenever you want to lose weight within a specific time, there is no better option than the keto diet. It is surely advantageous. Moreover, fats do not affect insulin in your body like carbohydrates do. So this would be beneficial for those people who had fallen prey to diabetes. There are also different forms of ketogenic diets which include the standard ketogenic diet, cyclic ketogenic diet, and targeted ketogenic diet. They are all different in nutrition content utilized to demonstrate diet plan.

# Benefits of Keto Diet - Is it for Everyone?

The ketogenic diet is full of benefits, which are listed below.

## Increases Mental Focus

On lowering carb intake, the blood sugar is lowered, and ketones are in action, which collectively enhances mental concentration by improving brain function.

## Helps in Weight Loss

As the body fats are utilized in the ketogenic diet, so an obvious weight loss is observed.

## Treats Epilepsy

Epilepsy was previously treated in the children by the keto diet, but now, adults are also being treated by this diet.

## Improves Blood Pressure and Cholesterol

The ketogenic diet helps in improving triglyceride and cholesterol levels. Many blood pressure issues are due to increased weight, so the keto diet helps in losing weight.

## Normalizes Hunger and Increases Energy

The most effective molecule to burn as a fuel is fat, so the ketogenic diet enhances our energy as it burns fat.

## Optimizes Insulin

The ketogenic diet helps in regulating the insulin levels, which prohibits diabetes.

## Treats Acne

The ketogenic diet improves skin problems by reducing skin inflammation and lesions.

## Controls Blood Sugar

The ketogenic diet is important in controlling blood sugar levels. It also controls diabetes this way.

# Breakfast Recipes

## Coconut Porridge

| Yield | Preparation Time | Cooking Time |
|---|---|---|
| 3 servings | 10 minutes | 3 minutes |

**Ingredients:**
- ¾ cup unsweetened, dried, coconut shreds
- 1 cup pecan halves
- 1 cup water
- 1 tablespoon yacon syrup
- 2 teaspoons melted coconut oil

**Directions:**
1. In a food processor, add the coconut shreds and pecans and pulse until an almond-meal-like mixture is formed.
2. Transfer the mixture into the pot of the Instant Pot and stir in the water, yacon syrup, and oil.
3. Secure the lid and place the pressure valve to the "Seal" position.
4. Select "Porridge" and just use the default time of 3 minutes.
5. Select "Cancel" and carefully do a "Quick" release.
6. Remove the lid and transfer into serving bowls.
7. Serve warm.

| Calories | Fat | Carbohydrates | Protein |
|---|---|---|---|
| 394 | 39.5 g | 11.2 g | 5.1 g |

## Chiles Quiche

| Yield | Preparation Time | Cooking Time |
|---|---|---|
| 4 servings | 15 minutes | 23 minutes |

- 1 cup shredded Mexican blend cheese, divided
- 1 cup half-and-half
- 4 organic eggs
- 10 ounces diced canned green chiles
- ½ teaspoon ground cumin
- Salt, to taste

**Directions:**
1. Arrange the trivet in the bottom of the Instant Pot and pour in two cups of water.
2. In a bowl, add half of the cheese and remaining ingredients and mix well.
3. Place the mixture into a generously greased 6-inch metal pan evenly.
4. Place the pan on top of the trivet.
5. Secure the lid and place the pressure valve to the "Seal" position.
6. Select "Manual" and cook under "High Pressure" for about 20 minutes.
7. Meanwhile, preheat the oven to broil.
8. Select "Cancel" and carefully do a "Natural" release for about 10 minutes, and then do a "Quick" release.
9. Remove the lid and transfer the pan onto the counter.
10. Sprinkle with the remaining cheese evenly and broil for about 2-3 minutes. Serve immediately.

| Calories | Fat | Carbohydrates | Protein |
|---|---|---|---|
| 289 | 21.3 grams | 9 grams | 14.5 grams |

## Spinach Quiche

| Yield | Preparation Time | Cooking Time |
|---|---|---|
| 8 servings | 15 minutes | 25 minutes |

**Ingredients:**

- ½ cup unsweetened almond milk
- 12 large organic eggs
- Salt and freshly ground black pepper, to taste
- 4 cups roughly chopped fresh baby spinach
- 3 large scallions, sliced
- 1 cup seeded and chopped tomato
- ½ cup shredded Parmesan cheese

**Directions:**

1. Arrange a steamer trivet in the bottom of the Instant Pot and pour in two cups of water.
2. In a large bowl, add the milk, eggs, salt, and black pepper and beat until well combined.
3. In another bowl, mix together the spinach, scallions, and tomato.
4. Transfer the spinach mixture into a 1 ½ quart baking dish.
5. Place the egg mixture over the spinach mixture and stir to combine.
6. Sprinkle with Parmesan cheese.
7. Place the baking dish on top of the trivet.
8. Secure the lid and place the pressure valve to the "Seal" position.
9. Select "Manual" and cook under "High Pressure" for about 20 minutes.

10. Meanwhile, preheat the oven to broil.
11. Select "Cancel" and carefully do a "Natural" release for about 10 minutes, and then do a "Quick" release.
12. Remove the lid and transfer the baking dish into the oven.
13. Broil for about 3-5 minutes.
14. Serve immediately.

**Nutrition Information per Serving:**

| Calories | Fat | Carbohydrates | Protein |
|---|---|---|---|
| 162 | 10.5 grams | 3.2 grams | 14.1 grams |

## Bacon & Egg Cups

| Yield | Preparation Time | Cooking Time |
|---|---|---|
| 4 servings | 10 minutes | 4 minutes |

- 1 tablespoon butter, melted
- 4 bacon slices
- 4 organic eggs
- 4 Gruyere cheese slices
- 2 tablespoons chopped tomato
- 1 teaspoon minced fresh cilantro

**Directions:**
1. Arrange a trivet in the bottom of the Instant Pot and pour 1 ½ cups of water in.
2. Grease four ramekins with melted butter and set aside.
3. Arrange one bacon slice in each prepared ramekin.
4. Carefully, crack one egg in each ramekin and top each with one cheese slice.
5. Place the ramekins on top of the trivet.
6. Secure the lid and place the pressure valve to the "Seal" position.
7. Select "Manual" and cook under "Low Pressure" for about 4 minutes.
8. Select the "Cancel" and carefully do a "Natural" release.
9. Remove the lid and serve immediately with the garnishing of tomato and cilantro.

| Calories | Fat | Carbohydrates | Protein |
|---|---|---|---|
| 362 | 28.4 grams | 1.1 grams | 24 grams |

## Veggie Muffins

| Yield | Preparation Time | Cooking Time |
|---|---|---|
| 6 servings | 15 minutes | 6 minutes |

**Ingredients:**
- 8 large eggs
- ¼ cup unsweetened almond milk
- ¼ teaspoon crushed red pepper flakes
- Salt and freshly ground black pepper, to taste
- 1 cup trimmed and chopped fresh kale
- ½ cup seeded and chopped tomato
- 2 scallions, sliced
- 1/3 cup shredded Parmesan cheese

**Directions:**
1. Arrange a steamer trivet in the bottom of the Instant Pot and pour in one cup of water.
2. Grease six (6 ounce) ovenproof custard cups.
3. In a large bowl, add the eggs, milk, red pepper flakes, salt, and black pepper and beat until well combined.
4. In another bowl, mix together the vegetables.
5. Divide the vegetable mixture into the prepared custard cups evenly and top with the egg mixture followed by the Parmesan cheese.
6. Place three custard cups on top of the trivet.

7. Now arrange the second trivet on top of the custard cups.
8. Place the remaining custard cups on top of the second trivet.
9. Secure the lid and place the pressure valve to the "Seal" position.
10. Select "Manual" and cook under "High Pressure" for about 6 minutes.
11. Select "Cancel" and carefully do a "Natural" release for about 5 minutes, and then do a "Quick" release.
12. Remove the lid and set the custard cups onto a wire rack to cool for about 10 minutes.
13. Carefully invert the muffins onto serving plates and serve warm.

**Nutrition Information per Serving:**

| Calories | Fat | Carbohydrates | Protein |
|---|---|---|---|
| 166 | 10.5 grams | 3.6 grams | 14.3 grams |

## Scallion Omelet

| Yield | Preparation Time | Cooking Time |
|---|---|---|
| 1 serving | 10 minutes | 5 minutes |

**Ingredients:**
- 1 large organic egg
- 1/3 cup water
- Pinch of garlic powder
- Salt and freshly ground black pepper, to taste
- 1 scallion, chopped
- Pinch of sesame seeds

**Directions:**
1. Arrange a steamer trivet in the bottom of the Instant Pot and pour in one cup of water.
2. In a heatproof bowl, add the egg, water, garlic powder, salt, and black pepper and beat until well combined.
3. Stir in scallion and sesame seeds.
4. Place the bowl on top of the trivet.
5. Secure the lid and place the pressure valve to the "Seal" position.
6. Select "Manual" and cook under "Manual" and "High Pressure" for about 5 minutes.
7. Select "Cancel" and carefully do a "Quick" release.
8. Remove the lid and serve immediately.

| Calories | Fat | Carbohydrates | Protein |
|---|---|---|---|
| 80 | 5.2 grams | 1.8 grams | 6.7 grams |

## Mushroom Omelet

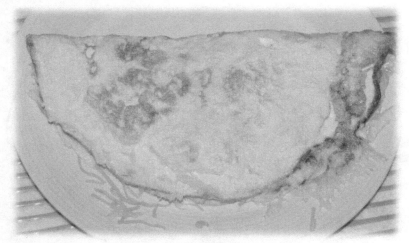

| Yield | Preparation Time | Cooking Time |
|---|---|---|
| 3 servings | 10 minutes | 5 minutes |

- 4 organic eggs
- 2 tablespoons unsweetened almond milk
- Salt and freshly ground black pepper, to taste
- 2 ½ tablespoons butter, divided
- ¾ cup chopped fresh mushrooms
- 3 tablespoons shredded mozzarella cheese

**Directions:**
1. In a large bowl, add the eggs, almond milk, salt, and black pepper and beat until well combined. Stir in the spinach.
2. Place one tablespoon of the butter in the Instant Pot and select "Sauté." Then add the mushrooms and cook for about 6-8 minutes.
3. Transfer the mushrooms into a bowl.
4. In the pot, add the remaining butter and melt it.
5. Select the "Cancel" button and place the egg mixture inside.
6. Secure the lid and place the pressure valve to the "Seal" position.
7. Select "Steam" and just use the default time of 5 minutes.
8. Select "Cancel" and carefully do a "Quick" release.
9. Remove the lid and transfer the omelet onto a plate.
10. Place the cheese over one half of the omelet and fold it.
11. Serve immediately.

| Calories | Fat | Carbohydrates | Protein |
|---|---|---|---|
| 254 | 20.6 grams | 2.1 grams | 16.1 grams |

## Bacon & Kale Casserole

| Yield | Preparation Time | Cooking Time |
|---|---|---|
| 6 servings | 15 minutes | 20 minutes |

- 6 organic eggs
- ½ cup heavy cream
- 1 cup shredded cheddar cheese
- 1 cup chopped cooked bacon
- 1 cup trimmed and chopped fresh kale leaves
- 1 small onion, chopped
- 1 teaspoon Herbs de Provence
- Salt and freshly ground black pepper, to taste

**Directions:**
1. Arrange a trivet in the bottom of the Instant Pot and pour in one cup of water.
2. In a large bowl, add the eggs and heavy cream and beat until well combined.
3. Add the remaining ingredients and mix well.
4. Place the mixture into a baking dish evenly.
5. Place the dish on top of the trivet.
6. Secure the lid, and place the pressure valve to the "Seal" position.
7. Select "Manual" and cook under "High Pressure" for about 20 minutes.
8. Select "Cancel" and carefully do a "Natural" release.
9. Serve immediately.

| Calories | Fat | Carbohydrates | Protein |
|---|---|---|---|
| 388 | 30.1 grams | 3.7 grams | 24.9 grams |

## Sweet Potato Casserole

| Yield | Preparation Time | Cooking Time |
|---|---|---|
| 4 servings | 25 minutes | 20 minutes |

**Ingredients:**

- 4 ounces sweet potatoes, peeled and cut into thin strips
- 6 large organic eggs
- 1 teaspoon Italian seasoning
- Salt and freshly ground black pepper, to taste
- ¼ cup unsweetened almond milk
- 2 tablespoons almond flour
- 1 teaspoon sugar-free tomato paste
- 1 tablespoon butter, melted
- ¼ cup chopped yellow onion
- 1 garlic clove, minced
- 6 ounces cheddar cheese, grated and divided

**Directions:**

1. Arrange a steamer trivet in the bottom of the Instant Pot and pour in 1 ½ cups of water.

2. Grease a casserole dish generously that will fit into the Instant Pot. Keep aside.
3. In a bowl, add eggs, seasonings, salt, and black pepper and beat until very frothy.
4. In another bowl, add the almond milk, flour, and tomato paste and beat until well combined.
5. Add the milk mixture into the egg mixture and beat until well combined.
6. Add the onion and garlic and stir to combine.
7. Add the sweet potato strips and butter into the bowl of milk mixture and stir to combine.
8. Transfer the mixture into the prepared casserole dish and top with the egg mixture, followed by four ounces of cheese.
9. Place the casserole dish on top of the trivet.
10. Secure the lid and place the pressure valve to the "Seal" position.
11. Select "Manual" and cook under "High Pressure" for about 15-20 minutes.
12. Select "Cancel" and carefully do a "Natural" release.
13. Remove the lid and immediately sprinkle with remaining cheese.
14. Secure the lid until the cheese is melted before serving.

**Nutrition Information per Serving:**

| Calories | Fat | Carbohydrates | Protein |
|---|---|---|---|
| 356 | 25.9 grams | 11 grams | 20.4 grams |

## Veggie Casserole

| Yield | Preparation Time | Cooking Time |
|---|---|---|
| 8 servings | 10 minutes | 2 minutes |

**Ingredients:**

- ½ cup unsweetened almond milk
- ¼ cup almond flour
- 8 large organic eggs
- Salt and freshly ground black pepper, to taste
- 1 cup chopped tomato
- 1 small zucchini, chopped
- 1 small green bell pepper, seeded and chopped
- 2 large scallions, chopped
- 2 cups shredded mozzarella cheese, divided

**Directions:**

1. Arrange the trivet in the bottom of the Instant Pot and pour in one cup of water.
2. In a heatproof bowl, add the almond milk, flour, eggs, salt, and black pepper and beat until well combined.
3. Add vegetables and one cup of cheese and stir to combine.
4. With a piece of foil, cover the bowl and place on top of the trivet.

5. Secure the lid and place the pressure valve to the "Seal" position.
6. Select "Manual" and cook under "High Pressure" for about 30 minutes.
7. Select "Cancel" and carefully do a "Natural" release for about 10 minutes, and then do a "Quick" release.
8. Remove the lid and immediately sprinkle with the remaining cheese.
9. Secure the lid until the cheese is melted completely.
10. Serve immediately.

**Nutrition Information per Serving:**

| Calories | Fat | Carbohydrates | Protein |
|---|---|---|---|
| 149 | 10.5 grams | 4.7 grams | 9.5 grams |

# Starter & Snack Recipes

## Scotch Eggs

| Yield | Preparation Time | Cooking Time |
|---|---|---|
| 4 servings | 15 minutes | 16 minutes |

**Ingredients:**

- 4 large organic eggs
- 1 pound gluten-free, country-style ground sausage
- 1 tablespoon olive oil

**Directions:**

1. Arrange a steamer basket in the bottom of the Instant Pot and pour in one cup of water.
2. Place the eggs into the steamer basket.
3. Secure the lid and place the pressure valve to the "Seal" position.
4. Select "Manual" and cook under "High Pressure" for about 6 minutes.
5. Select "Cancel" and carefully do a "Quick" release.
6. Remove the lid and transfer the eggs into a bowl of cold water to cool completely.
7. After cooling, peel the eggs.

8. Divide the sausage into 4 equal sized portions and flatten each into an oval-shaped patty.
9. Place 1 egg in the middle of each patty and gently mold the meat around it.
10. Remove the steamer basket and water from the Instant Pot.
11. With paper towels, pat dry the pot.
12. Place the oil in the Instant Pot and select "Sauté." Then add the scotch eggs and cook for about 3-4 minutes or until golden brown from all sides.
13. Transfer the scotch eggs onto a plate.
14. Arrange a steamer trivet in the bottom of the Instant Pot and pour in one cup of water.
15. Place the scotch eggs on top of the trivet.
16. Secure the lid and place the pressure valve to the "Seal" position.
17. Select "Manual" and cook under "High Pressure" for about 6 minutes.
18. Select "Cancel" and carefully do a "Quick" release.
19. Remove the lid and serve immediately.

**Nutrition Information per Serving:**

| Calories | Fat | Carbohydrates | Protein |
|---|---|---|---|
| 486 | 41.6 grams | 0.4 grams | 28.3 grams |

## Bacon Wrapped Asparagus

| Yield | Preparation Time | Cooking Time |
|---|---|---|
| 4 servings | 15 minutes | 3 minutes |

- 1 pound asparagus spears
- 8 ounces bacon slices

**Directions:**
1. Wrap the bacon slices around the asparagus spears.
2. In the bottom of the Instant Pot, arrange a steamer basket, and pour in two cups of water.
3. Arrange any extra un-wrapped spears in the bottom of the steamer basket in a single layer.
4. Place the wrapped asparagus on top in a single layer.
5. Secure the lid and place the pressure valve to the "Seal" position.
6. Select "Manual" and cook under "High Pressure" for about 2-3 minutes.
7. Select "Cancel" and carefully do a "Natural" release.
8. Remove the lid and serve warm

| Calories | Fat | Carbohydrates | Protein |
|---|---|---|---|
| 329 | 39.5 grams | 23.8 grams | 23.5 grams |

## Buffalo Chicken Dip

| Yield | Preparation Time | Cooking Time |
|---|---|---|
| 10 servings | 15 minutes | 10 minutes |

**Ingredients:**

- 2 (4 ounce) grass-fed skinless, boneless chicken breasts
- ½ cup sugar-free buffalo sauce
- ¼ cup water
- 6 ounces cream cheese, softened
- Salt and freshly ground black pepper, to taste

**Directions:**

1. In the pot of the Instant Pot, place the chicken breasts, buffalo sauce and water and stir to combine.
2. Secure the lid and place the pressure valve to the "Seal" position.
3. Select "Manual" and cook under "High Pressure" for about 8-10 minutes.
4. Select "Cancel" and carefully do a "Natural" release.
5. Remove the lid and transfer the chicken breasts onto a plate.
6. With two forks, shred the chicken.
7. In the pot, add the shredded chicken and remaining ingredients and stir to combine well.
8. Serve immediately.

| Calories | Fat | Carbohydrates | Protein |
|---|---|---|---|
| 88 | 6.7 grams | 0.5 grams | 6.7 grams |

## Boiled Peanuts

| Yield | Preparation Time | Cooking Time |
|---|---|---|
| 6 servings | 10 minutes | 1 ½ hours |

**Ingredients:**
- 1 pound jumbo raw peanuts
- ½ cup sea salt
- 1 tablespoon Cajun seasoning

**Directions:**
1. Rinse the peanuts under cold running water and remove any twigs and roots.
2. In the pot of the Instant Pot, place in all of the ingredients and enough water to cover the peanuts and stir.
3. Place a plate or trivet on top of the peanuts.
4. Secure the lid and place the pressure valve to the "Seal" position.
5. Select "Manual" and cook under "High Pressure" for about 65-90 minutes.
6. Select "Cancel" and carefully do a "Natural" release.
7. Remove the lid and keep aside to cool.
8. Drain well and serve.

| Calories | Fat | Carbohydrates | Protein |
|---|---|---|---|
| 429 | 37.2 grams | 12 grams | 19.5 grams |

**Roasted Pecans**

| Yield | Preparation Time | Cooking Time |
|---|---|---|
| 30 servings | 10 minutes | 12 minutes |

- 1 teaspoon butter
- 4 cups raw pecans
- ¼ cup Swerve
- 1 teaspoon ground cinnamon
- Pinch of salt

**Directions:**
1. Place the butter in the Instant Pot and select "Sauté." Then add all of the ingredients except water and cook for about 5 minutes, stirring frequently.
2. Select "Cancel" and stir in about ½ a cup of water.
3. Secure the lid and place the pressure valve to the "Seal" position.
4. Select "Manual" and cook under "High Pressure" for about 10 minutes.
5. Meanwhile, preheat the oven to 350 degrees F.
6. Select "Cancel" and carefully do a "Natural" release for about 10 minutes, and then do a "Quick" release.
7. Remove the lid and transfer the pecans onto a baking sheet.
8. Bake for about 5 minutes.
9. Remove from oven and keep aside to cool before serving.

| Calories | Fat | Carbohydrates | Protein |
|---|---|---|---|
| 117 | 12 grams | 4.9 grams | 1.8 grams |

# Soup Recipes

## Onion Soup

| Yield | Preparation Time | Cooking Time |
|---|---|---|
| 4 servings | 15 minutes | 13 minutes |

- ¼ cup unsalted butter
- 5 yellow onions, sliced
- 6 cups homemade vegetable broth
- Salt and freshly ground black pepper, to taste
- ¼ cup shredded Gruyere cheese

**Directions:**
1. Place the butter in the Instant Pot and select "Sauté." Then add the onion and cook for about 3 minutes.
2. Select "Cancel" and stir in the broth, salt, and black pepper.
3. Secure the lid and place the pressure valve to the "Seal" position.
4. Select "Manual" and cook under "High Pressure" for about 10 minutes.
5. Select "Cancel" and carefully do a "Natural" release.
6. Remove the lid and serve hot with the topping of cheese.

**Nutrition Information per Serving:**

| Calories | Fat | Carbohydrates | Protein |
|---|---|---|---|
| 242 | 15 grams | 13 grams | 10.9 grams |

## Pumpkin Soup

| Yield | Preparation Time | Cooking Time |
|---|---|---|
| 6 servings | 15 minutes | 8 minutes |

**Ingredients:**
- 15 ounces canned pumpkin
- 3 ½ ounces homemade vegetable broth
- 13 ½ ounces unsweetened coconut milk
- ¼ cup creamy peanut butter
- Salt and freshly ground black pepper, to taste

**Directions:**
1. In the pot of the Instant Pot, place in all of the ingredients and stir to combine.
2. Secure the lid and place the pressure valve to the "Seal" position.
3. Select "Manual" and cook under "High Pressure" for about 15 minutes.
4. Select "Cancel" and carefully do a "Natural" release.
5. Remove the lid and stir well.
6. Serve immediately.

**Nutrition Information per Serving:**

| Calories | Fat | Carbohydrates | Protein |
|---|---|---|---|
| 246 | 21.2 grams | 11 grams | 6.2 grams |

## Broccoli Soup

| Yield | Preparation Time | Cooking Time |
|---|---|---|
| 6 servings | 15 minutes | 13 minutes |

**Ingredients:**

- 2 tablespoons butter
- 2 small carrots, peeled and chopped
- 1 small yellow onion, chopped
- 2 tablespoons almond flour
- 1 garlic clove, minced
- 3 cups homemade vegetable broth
- 5 cups broccoli florets
- 1 teaspoon dill weed
- 1 teaspoon smoked paprika
- Salt and freshly ground black pepper, to taste
- 4 American cheese slices, cut into pieces
- 1 cup shredded Colby Jack cheese
- 1 cup shredded Pepper Jack cheese
- ½ cup shredded Parmesan cheese
- 1 cup half-and-half

**Directions:**

1. Place the butter in the Instant Pot and select "Sauté." Then add the carrot and onion and cook for about 2-3 minutes.
2. Stir in the flour and garlic and cook for about 1 minute, stirring continuously.
3. Stir in broth and cook for about 1 minute or until smooth, stirring continuously.
4. Select "Cancel" and stir in the broccoli.
5. Secure the lid and place the pressure valve to the "Seal" position.
6. Select "Manual" and cook under "High Pressure" for about 8 minutes.
7. Select "Cancel" and carefully do a "Quick" release.
8. Remove the lid and immediately stir in the dill weed, paprika, salt, and black pepper.
9. Add cheeses and half-and-half and stir until melted and well combined.
10. Serve immediately.

**Nutrition Information per Serving:**

| Calories | Fat | Carbohydrates | Protein |
|---|---|---|---|
| 372 | 27.3 grams | 12 grams | 19.8 grams |

## Carrot Soup

| Yield | Preparation Time | Cooking Time |
|---|---|---|
| 6 servings | 15 minutes | 40 minutes |

**Ingredients:**

- 2 tablespoons butter
- 1 small yellow onion, chopped
- 1 garlic clove, minced
- 1 pound carrots, peeled and chopped
- 1 tablespoon curry powder
- Salt and freshly ground black pepper, to taste
- 1 (14 ounce) can unsweetened coconut milk
- 3 cups homemade chicken broth
- ½ cup sour cream

**Directions:**

1. Place the butter in the Instant Pot and select "Sauté." Then add the onion and garlic and cook for about 3 minutes.
2. Add the garlic and cook for about 1 minute.
3. Add the carrots, curry powder, salt, and black pepper and cook for about 2 minutes.
4. Select "Cancel" and stir in the coconut milk, broth, and Sriracha sauce.

5. Secure the lid and place the pressure valve to the "Seal" position.
6. Select "Manual" and cook under "High Pressure" for about 6 minutes.
7. Select "Cancel" and carefully do a "Natural" release for about 10 minutes and then do a "Quick" release.
8. Remove the lid, and with an immersion blender, puree the soup.
9. Serve immediately with the topping of sour cream.

**Nutrition Information per Serving:**

| Calories | Fat | Carbohydrates | Protein |
|---|---|---|---|
| 265 | 20.4 grams | 11 grams | 11 grams |

## Cauliflower Soup

| Yield | Preparation Time | Cooking Time |
|---|---|---|
| 6 servings | 15 minutes | 8 minutes |

**Ingredients:**
- 2 ½ pounds cauliflower, chopped
- ½ yellow onion, chopped
- 2 cups homemade chicken broth
- Salt and freshly ground black pepper, to taste
- 10 ounces cream cheese, softened

**Directions:**
1. In the pot of the Instant Pot, place in all of the ingredients except cream cheese and stir to combine.
2. Secure the lid and place the pressure valve to the "Seal" position.
3. Select "Manual" and cook under "High Pressure" for about 8 minutes.
4. Select "Cancel" and carefully do a "Quick" release.
5. Remove the lid and stir in the cream cheese.
6. With an immersion blender, blend the soup until it's smooth.
7. Serve immediately.

**Nutrition Information per Serving:**

| Calories | Fat | Carbohydrates | Protein |
|---|---|---|---|
| 229 | 17.1 grams | 11 grams | 9 grams |

## Bacon & Veggie Soup

| Yield | Preparation Time | Cooking Time |
|---|---|---|
| 6 servings | 15 minutes | 23 minutes |

- 1 tablespoon butter
- 1 small yellow onion, chopped
- 2 garlic cloves, minced
- 1 head cauliflower, chopped roughly
- 1 red bell pepper, seeded and chopped
- Salt and freshly ground black pepper, to taste
- 4 cups homemade chicken broth
- 2 cups shredded cheddar cheese
- 1 cup half-and-half
- 6 cooked turkey bacon slices, chopped
- 4 dashes hot pepper sauce

**Directions:**
1. Place the butter in the Instant Pot and select "Sauté." Then add the onion and garlic and cook for about 3 minutes.
2. Select "Cancel" and stir in the cauliflower, bell pepper, salt, black pepper, and broth.
3. Secure the lid and place the pressure valve to the "Seal" position.
4. Select "Soup" and just use the default time of 15 minutes.
5. Select "Cancel" and carefully do a "Quick" release.
6. Remove the lid and stir in the remaining ingredients.
7. Select "Sauté" and cook for about 5 minutes. Serve immediately

| Calories | Fat | Carbohydrates | Protein |
|---|---|---|---|
| 427 | 32.2 grams | 8.5 grams | 25.8 grams |

### Cheeseburger Soup

| Yield | Preparation Time | Cooking Time |
|---|---|---|
| 8 servings | 15 minutes | 20 minutes |

- 1 tablespoon butter
- 2 pounds grass-fed ground beef
- 4 garlic cloves, minced
- 2 tablespoons red chili powder
- 2 teaspoons ground cumin
- 20 ounces canned diced tomatoes with green chiles
- 4 cups water
- Salt and freshly ground black pepper, to taste
- 8 ounce cream cheese, softened
- ½ cup heavy cream

**Directions:**
1. Place the butter in the Instant Pot and select "Sauté." Then add the beef and cook for about 10 minutes or until browned completely.
2. Select "Cancel" and stir in the remaining ingredients except cream cheese and cream and stir to combine.
3. Secure the lid and place the pressure valve to the "Seal" position.
4. Select the "Soup" setting and just use the default time of 10 minutes.
5. Select "Cancel" and carefully do a "Natural" release.
6. Remove the lid and stir in the cream cheese and cream until smooth.
7. Serve hot.

| Calories | Fat | Carbohydrates | Protein |
|---|---|---|---|
| 389 | 27 grams | 5.5 grams | 28.1 grams |

## Chicken Soup

| Yield | Preparation Time | Cooking Time |
|---|---|---|
| 5 servings | 15 minutes | 12 minutes |

- 2 tablespoons olive oil
- 2 celery stalks, chopped
- 2 carrots, peeled and chopped
- 1 small yellow onion, chopped
- ¼ teaspoon crushed dried oregano
- ¼ teaspoon crushed dried thyme
- Salt and freshly ground black pepper, to taste
- 4 cups homemade chicken broth
- 1 cup water
- 1 pound grass-fed cooked chicken, chopped
- 2 cups trimmed and chopped finely fresh kale

**Directions:**
1. Place the oil in the Instant Pot and select "Sauté." Then add the celery, carrot, and onion and cook for about 5 minutes.
2. Add herbs and black pepper and cook for about 1 minute.
3. Select "Cancel" and stir in the broth and water.
4. Secure the lid and place the pressure valve to the "Seal" position.
5. Select "Soup" and just use the default time of 4 minutes.
6. Select "Cancel" and carefully do a "Quick" release.
7. Remove the lid and stir in the chicken and kale.
8. Select "Sauté" and cook for about 1-2 minutes more. Serve immediately.

| Calories | Fat | Carbohydrates | Protein |
|---|---|---|---|
| 246 | 9.5 grams | 7.5 grams | 31.4 grams |

## Creamy Chicken Soup

| Yield | Preparation Time | Cooking Time |
|---|---|---|
| 6 servings | 20 minutes | 40 minutes |

**Ingredients:**

- 6 (4 ounce) grass-fed boneless chicken thighs, cubed
- 6 ounces fresh mushrooms, chopped
- ½ cup chopped yellow onion
- ¼ cup chopped celery
- ¼ cup peeled and chopped carrot
- 4 tablespoons butter
- 1 teaspoon dried thyme
- Salt and freshly ground black pepper, to taste
- 3 cups homemade chicken broth
- 2 cups chopped fresh spinach
- 1 cup heavy cream

**Directions:**

1. In the pot of the Instant Pot, place in all of the ingredients except spinach and cream and stir to combine.
2. Secure the lid and place the pressure valve to the "Seal" position.

3. Select "Soup" and just use the default time of 30 minutes.
4. Select "Cancel" and carefully do a "Natural" release for about 10 minutes, and then do a "Quick" release.
5. Remove the lid and select "Sauté."
6. Stir in spinach and cream and cook for about 10 minutes.
7. Select "Cancel" and serve hot.

**Nutrition Information per Serving:**

| Calories | Fat | Carbohydrates | Protein |
|---|---|---|---|
| 412 | 33 grams | 3.9 grams | 24 grams |

## Meatballs Soup

| Yield | Preparation Time | Cooking Time |
|---|---|---|
| 6 servings | 20 minutes | 18 minutes |

**Ingredients:**

- 1 pound gluten-free hot Italian sausage, casing removed
- 1 tablespoon butter
- 2 carrots, peeled and sliced thinly
- 1 small yellow onion, chopped
- 1 garlic clove, chopped
- Salt and freshly ground black pepper, to taste
- 4 cups homemade chicken broth
- 2-3 cups fresh baby spinach leaves
- 4 tablespoons grated Parmesan cheese

**Directions:**

1. Make equal-sized meatballs from the sausage.
2. Place the butter in the Instant Pot and select "Sauté." Then add the carrots and onion and cook for about 2-3 minutes.
3. Select "Cancel" and stir in the meatballs, garlic, salt, black pepper, and broth.
4. Secure the lid and place the pressure valve to the "Seal" position.
5. Select "Manual" and cook under "High Pressure" for about 5 minutes.
6. Select "Cancel" and carefully do a "Natural" release for about 10 minutes and then do a "Quick" release.
7. Remove the lid and stir in the spinach.
8. Serve hot with the garnishing of Parmesan.

**Nutrition Information per Serving:**

| Calories | Fat | Carbohydrates | Protein |
|---|---|---|---|
| 336 | 25.5 grams | 4.7 grams | 20 grams |

# Meat Recipes

## Beef with Bell Peppers

| Yield | Preparation Time | Cooking Time |
|---|---|---|
| 5 servings | 15 minutes | 30 minutes |

- 2 tablespoons butter
- 1 pound grass-fed boneless beef, trimmed and sliced into thin strips
- Salt and freshly ground black pepper, to taste
- 2 cups finely chopped tomatoes
- 1 ½ cups sugar-free tomato sauce
- 3 garlic cloves, minced
- 1 teaspoon crushed dried rosemary
- 1 cup water
- 1 large green bell pepper, seeded and sliced into ½-inch thick strips
- 1 large red bell pepper, seeded and sliced into ½-inch thick strips
- 1 large yellow bell pepper, seeded and sliced into ½-inch thick strips

**Directions:**
1. Place the butter in the Instant Pot and select "Sauté." Then add the beef, a little salt, and black pepper, and cook for about 5 minutes.
2. Select "Cancel" and transfer the beef into a bowl.
3. Now add the tomatoes, tomato sauce, garlic, rosemary, salt, black pepper, and water and stir to combine.
4. Place the beef on top, followed by the bell peppers.
5. Secure the lid and place the pressure valve to the "Seal" position.
6. Select "Manual" and cook under "High Pressure" for about 25 minutes.
7. Select "Cancel" and carefully do a "Quick" release.
8. Remove the lid and serve hot.

| Calories | Fat | Carbohydrates | Protein |
|---|---|---|---|
| 444 | 38 grams | 11 grams | 15 grams |

## Shredded Chuck Roast

| Yield | Preparation Time | Cooking Time |
|---|---|---|
| 10 servings | 10 minutes | 1 hour 25 minutes |

**Ingredients:**

- 3 pounds grass-fed beef chuck roast, trimmed and cut into large chunks
- 1 large yellow onion, sliced
- 6 garlic cloves
- 2 (4 ounce) cans of green chilies
- 1 tablespoon dried oregano
- Salt and freshly ground black pepper, to taste
- ¼ cup fresh lime juice
- ¾ cup water
- 2 tablespoons butter

**Directions:**

1. In the pot of the Instant Pot, add all of the ingredients and stir to combine.
2. Secure the lid and place the pressure valve to the "Seal" position.
3. Select "Manual" and cook under "High Pressure" for about 1 hour.
4. Select "Cancel" and carefully do a "Natural" release.
5. Remove the lid and transfer the roast onto a plate.
6. With two forks, shred the meat and return it into the Instant Pot alongside the butter.
7. Now select "Sauté" and cook for about 20-25 minutes or until the desired doneness of sauce.
8. Select "Cancel" and serve hot.

**Nutrition Information per Serving:**

| Calories | Fat | Carbohydrates | Protein |
|---|---|---|---|
| 531 | 40.3 grams | 3.6 grams | 36.1 grams |

## Braised Chuck Roast

| Yield | Preparation Time | Cooking Time |
|---|---|---|
| 6 servings | 15 minutes | 50 minutes |

**Ingredients:**

**For Roast:**

- 2 tablespoons ground coffee
- 1 tablespoon cacao powder
- 1 tablespoon smoked paprika
- 1 teaspoon ground ginger
- ½ teaspoon ground garlic
- 1 teaspoon red chili powder
- 1 teaspoon red pepper flakes
- Salt and freshly ground black pepper, to taste
- 2 pounds grass-fed beef chuck roast, trimmed and cut into 1 ½-inch cubes
- 3 tablespoons butter

**For Sauce:**

- 1 cup homemade beef broth
- ½ cup brewed coffee
- 1 medium yellow onion, chopped
- 2 tablespoon fresh lemon juice
- Salt and freshly ground black pepper, to taste

**Directions:**

1. For the roast: in a small bowl, add all of the ingredients, except the roast and butter and mix well.
2. Rub the chuck roast with the spice mixture generously.
3. For the sauce: in a food processor, add all of the ingredients and pulse until smooth.
4. Place the butter in the Instant Pot and select "Sauté." Then add the beef and cook for about 10 minutes or until browned completely.
5. Select "Cancel" and top the roast with sauce evenly.
6. Secure the lid and place the pressure valve to the "Seal" position.
7. Select "Manual" and cook under "High Pressure" for about 35-40 minutes.
8. Select "Cancel" and carefully do a "Natural" release.
9. Remove the lid and transfer the roast onto a platter.
10. Top with the sauce and serve.

**Nutrition Information per Serving:**

| Calories | Fat | Carbohydrates | Protein |
|----------|-----|---------------|---------|
| 624 | 48.6 grams | 3.8 grams | 41.2 grams |

## Beef Short Ribs

| Yield | Preparation Time | Cooking Time |
|---|---|---|
| 8 servings | 15 minutes | 1 hour 3 minutes |

**Ingredients:**

- ½ cup almond flour
- Salt and freshly ground black pepper, to taste
- 3 ¼ pounds grass-fed beef short ribs
- 3 tablespoons unsalted butter, divided
- 1 small yellow onion, chopped
- 2 garlic cloves, minced
- 1 tablespoon fresh rosemary, chopped
- ½ cup homemade beef broth

**Directions:**

1. In a large bowl, mix together the almond flour, salt, and black pepper.
2. Add the beef ribs and coat with the flour mixture generously. Shake off the excess mixture.

3. Place one tablespoon of butter in the Instant Pot and select "Sauté." Then add the ribs and cook for about 6-8 minutes or until browned completely.
4. Transfer the beef ribs into a bowl.
5. Add the remaining butter and onion and cook for about 2-3 minutes.
6. Add the garlic and rosemary and cook for about 1 minute.
7. Stir in the broth and water and cook for about 1 minute.
8. Select "Cancel" and stir in the beef ribs.
9. Secure the lid and place the pressure valve to the "Seal" position.
10. Select "Manual" and cook under "High Pressure" for about 50 minutes.
11. Select "Cancel" and carefully do a "Quick" release.
12. Remove the lid and transfer ribs onto a serving platter.
13. Top with the cooking liquid and serve.

**Nutrition Information per Serving:**

| Calories | Fat | Carbohydrates | Protein |
| --- | --- | --- | --- |
| 466 | 24.5 grams | 2.9 grams | 55.2 grams |

**Beef Curry**

| Yield | Preparation Time | Cooking Time |
|---|---|---|
| 8 servings | 15 minutes | 38 minutes |

**Ingredients:**

- 3 tablespoons coconut oil
- 2 pounds grass-fed beef stew meat, cut into 1-inch pieces
- Salt and freshly ground black pepper, to taste
- 1 cup chopped yellow onion
- 1 tablespoon minced fresh ginger
- 2 teaspoons minced garlic
- 1 jalapeño pepper, chopped
- 1 tablespoon curry powder
- 1 teaspoon red chili powder
- 1 teaspoon ground cumin
- 1 tablespoon sugar-free tomato sauce
- 2 cups homemade beef broth
- 1 ½ cups peeled and cut into 1-inch pieces carrots
- 2 cups canned unsweetened coconut milk
- ½ cup chopped fresh parsley

**Directions:**

1. Place the coconut oil in the Instant Pot and select "Sauté." Then add the beef in batches with the salt and black pepper and cook for about 4-5 minutes or until browned completely, stirring frequently.
2. Transfer the beef into a bowl.
3. In the pot, add the onion, ginger, garlic, and jalapeño pepper and cook for about 4-5 minutes.
4. Select "Cancel" and stir in the beef, spices, and broth.
5. Secure the lid and place the pressure valve to the "Seal" position.
6. Select "Manual" and cook under "High Pressure" for about 15 minutes.
7. Select "Cancel" and carefully do a "Quick" release.
8. Remove the lid and stir in the carrots.
9. Select "Manual" and cook under "High Pressure" for about 5 minutes.
10. Select "Cancel" and carefully do a "Natural" release for about 10 minutes, and then do a "Quick" release.
11. Remove the lid and stir in the coconut milk.
12. Select "Sauté" and cook for about 2-3 minutes.
13. Select "Cancel" and serve immediately with the garnishing of parsley.

**Nutrition Information per Serving:**

| Calories | Fat | Carbohydrates | Protein |
|---|---|---|---|
| 427 | 27.1 grams | 8.8 grams | 37.8 grams |

## Beef with Mushroom Sauce

| Yield | Preparation Time | Cooking Time |
|---|---|---|
| 12 servings | 20 minutes | 1 hour 7 minutes |

### Ingredients:

- 3 ½ pounds grass-fed sirloin tip roast, trimmed and cubed
- ½ teaspoon crushed dried rosemary
- ½ teaspoon crushed dried thyme
- ½ teaspoon onion powder
- Salt and freshly ground white pepper, to taste
- 3 tablespoons butter
- 1 medium yellow onion, chopped
- 3 cups fresh mushrooms, sliced
- 3 garlic cloves, minced
- 3 cups homemade beef broth
- 16 ounces sour cream

**Directions:**

1. In a bowl, add the beef, herbs, onion powder, salt, and white pepper and toss to coat well.
2. Place the butter in the Instant Pot and select "Sauté." Then add the beef in batches and cook for about 4-5 minutes or until browned.
3. Transfer the beef into a bowl.
4. Now add the onion and sauté for about 3-4 minutes.
5. Add the mushrooms and sauté for about 4-5 minutes.
6. Add garlic and sauté for about 1 minute.
7. Select "Cancel" and stir in the cooked beef and broth.
8. Secure the lid and place the pressure valve to the "Seal" position.
9. Select "Manual" and cook under "High Pressure" for about 20 minutes.
10. Select "Cancel" and carefully do a "Natural" release.
11. Remove the lid and transfer about ½ cup of cooking liquid into a bowl.
12. Add the sour cream and stir until cream becomes warm enough.
13. Add the cream and required amount of salt and black pepper in the pot and stir to combine.
14. Serve hot.

**Nutrition Information per Serving:**

| Calories | Fat | Carbohydrates | Protein |
|---|---|---|---|
| 366 | 22.2 grams | 3.7 grams | 38 grams |

## Beef with Broccoli

| Yield | Preparation Time | Cooking Time |
|---|---|---|
| 5 servings | 15 minutes | 32 minutes |

**Ingredients:**

- 2 tablespoons butter
- 1 pound grass-fed beef chuck roast, trimmed and cut into thin strips
- Salt and freshly ground black pepper, to taste
- 1 small yellow onion, chopped
- 2 garlic cloves, minced
- Pinch of crushed red pepper flakes
- ½ cup homemade beef broth
- ¼ cup low-sodium soy sauce
- 1 tablespoon Erythritol
- 1 tablespoon arrowroot starch
- 1 ½ tablespoons cold water
- ¾ pound broccoli florets
- 2 tablespoons water
- 2 tablespoons chopped fresh cilantro

**Directions:**

1. Place the butter in the Instant Pot and select "Sauté." Then add the beef, salt, and black pepper and cook for about 5 minutes.
2. Transfer the beef into a bowl.
3. Now add the onion and cook for about 4-5 minutes.
4. Add the garlic and red pepper flakes and cook for about 1 minute.
5. Add the broth, soy sauce, and Erythritol and stir well.
6. Select "Cancel" and stir in the beef.
7. Secure the lid and place the pressure valve to the "Seal" position.
8. Select "Manual" and cook under "High Pressure" for about 12 minutes.
9. Select "Cancel" and carefully do a "Quick" release.
10. Meanwhile, in a small bowl, dissolve the arrowroot starch in cold water.
11. Remove the lid and select "Sauté."
12. Add the arrowroot mixture in the Instant Pot, stirring continuously.
13. Cook for about 4-5 minutes or until desired thickness is reached.
14. Meanwhile, in a large microwave-safe bowl, add the broccoli and two tablespoons of water and microwave on High for about 3-4 minutes.
15. Add the broccoli into the Instant Pot and stir well.
16. Select "Cancel" and serve hot.

**Nutrition Information per Serving:**

| Calories | Fat | Carbohydrates | Protein |
| --- | --- | --- | --- |
| 414 | 30.2 grams | 8.6 grams | 27.2 grams |

## Ground Beef Curry

| Yield | Preparation Time | Cooking Time |
|---|---|---|
| 6 servings | 10 minutes | 43 minutes |

**Ingredients:**

- 2 tablespoons coconut oil
- 2 medium carrots, peeled and chopped finely
- 2 celery stalks, chopped finely
- 1 small yellow onion, chopped finely
- Salt, to taste
- 2 ¼ pounds grass-fed ground beef
- 4 garlic cloves, chopped finely
- 2 tablespoons low-sodium soy sauce
- 1 teaspoon fish sauce
- 1 teaspoon paprika
- ½ teaspoon ground cinnamon
- 2 (14 ounce) cans sugar-free diced tomatoes with juice
- ½ cup heavy whipping cream

**Directions:**

1. Place the oil in the Instant Pot and select "Sauté." Then add the carrot, celery and onion and cook for about 5 minutes.
2. Add the beef and cook for about 2-3 minutes.
3. Add the garlic, both sauces, and spices and cook for about 5 minutes.
4. Select "Cancel" and stir in the tomatoes with juice.
5. Secure the lid and place the pressure valve to the "Seal" position.
6. Select "Manual" and cook under "High Pressure" for about 20 minutes.
7. Select "Cancel" and carefully do a "Natural" release.
8. Remove the lid and select "Sauté."
9. Cook for about 5-10 minutes or until desired thickness of sauce.
10. Select "Cancel" and stir in sour cream.
11. Serve hot.

**Nutrition Information per Serving:**

| Calories | Fat | Carbohydrates | Protein |
| --- | --- | --- | --- |
| 318 | 17.9 grams | 8 grams | 27 grams |

## Meatballs in Gravy

| Yield | Preparation Time | Cooking Time |
|---|---|---|
| 6 servings | 20 minutes | 39 minutes |

### Ingredients:

- 1 ½ pounds grass-fed lean ground beef
- 2 teaspoons adobo seasoning
- Salt and freshly ground black pepper, to taste
- 2 tablespoons olive butter
- 4 small tomatoes, chopped roughly
- 8 mini bell peppers, seeded and halved
- 1 small yellow onion, chopped roughly
- 4 garlic cloves, peeled
- 1 cup sugar-free tomato sauce
- ½ teaspoon crushed red pepper flakes

**Directions:**

1. In a bowl, add the beef, adobo seasoning, salt, and black pepper and mix well.
2. Make golf-ball-sized balls from the mixture.
3. Place the oil in the Instant Pot and select "Sauté." Then add the meatballs and cook for about 3-4 minutes or until browned completely.
4. Select "Cancel" and transfer the meatballs into a bowl.
5. In the pot of the Instant Pot, place the remaining ingredients in and top with the meatballs.
6. Secure the lid and place the pressure valve to the "Seal" position.
7. Select "Meat/Stew" and just use the default time of 35 minutes.
8. Select "Cancel" and carefully do a "Natural" release.
9. Remove the lid and, with a slotted spoon, transfer the meatballs onto a plate.
10. With an immersion blender, blend the vegetable mixture until smooth.
11. Add the meatballs, salt, and black pepper into the sauce and gently stir to combine.
12. Serve immediately.

**Nutrition Information per Serving:**

| Calories | Fat | Carbohydrates | Protein |
|---|---|---|---|
| 257 | 15 grams | 11 grams | 25.5 grams |

### Herbed Meatloaf

| Yield | Preparation Time | Cooking Time |
|---|---|---|
| 6 servings | 15 minutes | 28 minutes |

**Ingredients:**

**For Meatloaf:**

- 1 pound grass-fed lean ground beef
- ½ cup heavy cream
- 1 organic egg
- ½ cup almond flour
- ½ yellow onion, grated
- ½ teaspoon mustard powder
- 1 teaspoon garlic powder
- Salt and freshly ground black pepper, to taste

**For Topping:**

- 1 tablespoon sugar-free ketchup
- ½ tablespoon low-sodium soy sauce
- ½ tablespoon Swerve
- ½ tablespoon fresh lemon juice
- ¼ cup crumbled feta cheese

**Directions:**

1. For the meatloaf: in a bowl, add all of the ingredients and mix until well combined.
2. Arrange an 18x18-inch square piece of foil onto a smooth surface.
3. Arrange the meat mixture into the center of the foil and shape into a loaf.
4. Carefully fold the foil around the meatloaf.
5. Arrange a trivet in the bottom of the Instant Pot and pour in one cup of water.
6. Arrange the wrapped meatloaf on top of the trivet.
7. Secure the lid and place the pressure valve to the "Seal" position.
8. Select "Manual" and cook under "High Pressure" for about 25 minutes.
9. Meanwhile, preheat the oven to broil.
10. Select "Cancel" and carefully do a "Natural" release for about 10 minutes, and then do a "Quick" release.
11. Meanwhile, for the glaze: in a bowl, add all of the ingredients and mix until well combined.
12. Carefully, remove the meatloaf from foil and transfer onto a broiler pan.
13. Spread the glaze over meatloaf evenly.
14. Broil for about 2-3 minutes.
15. Remove from the oven and immediately top with the feta cheese.
16. Cut into desired sized slices and serve.

**Nutrition Information per Serving:**

| Calories | Fat | Carbohydrates | Protein |
|---|---|---|---|
| 258 | 17.2 grams | 4.8 grams | 19 grams |

## BBQ Pork Ribs

| Yield | Preparation Time | Cooking Time |
|---|---|---|
| 6 servings | 15 minutes | 30 minutes |

**Ingredients:**

- 2 pounds pork baby back ribs
- 2 bay leaves
- 4 garlic cloves, minced
- 2 tablespoons Italian seasoning
- Salt and freshly ground black pepper, to taste
- 4 cups water
- ½ cup sugar-free BBQ sauce

**Directions:**

1. In the pot of the Instant Pot, add all of the ingredients except the BBQ sauce and stir to combine.
2. Secure the lid and place the pressure valve to the "Seal" position.
3. Select "Manual" and cook under "High Pressure" for about 20 minutes.
4. Select "Cancel" and carefully do a "Natural" release.
5. Remove the lid and transfer the pork ribs onto a cutting board for about 5 minutes.
6. With paper towels, pat dry the ribs completely.
7. Transfer the ribs into a bowl. Add the BBQ sauce and coat the ribs with sauce generously.
8. Cover and refrigerate for about 2-3 hours.
9. Preheat the oven to broil.
10. Broil the ribs for about 5 minutes per side.
11. Serve immediately.

**Nutrition Information per Serving:**

| Calories | Fat | Carbohydrates | Protein |
|---|---|---|---|
| 600 | 46.5 grams | 12 grams | 34.4 grams |

## Pork Chops

| Yield | Preparation Time | Cooking Time |
|---|---|---|
| 4 servings | 10 minutes | 13 minutes |

- 4 (6 ounce) bone-in pork loin chops
- Salt and freshly ground black pepper, to taste
- 2 tablespoons butter
- 1 cup homemade chicken broth
- 1 tablespoon chopped fresh parsley

**Directions:**
1. Season the pork chops with salt and black pepper evenly.
2. Place the butter in the Instant Pot and select "Sauté." Then add the pork chops and cook for about 3-4 minutes per side.
3. Select "Cancel" and transfer the chops onto a plate.
4. In the pot, add the broth and scrape the brown bits from the bottom.
5. Arrange a trivet in the bottom of the Instant Pot.
6. Place the pork chops on top of the trivet.
7. Secure the lid and place the pressure valve to the "Seal" position.
8. Select "Meat/Stew" and just use the default time of 5 minutes.
9. Select "Cancel" and carefully do a "Natural" release for about 5 minutes, and then do a "Quick" release.
10. Remove the lid and serve hot with the garnishing of parsley.

| Calories | Fat | Carbohydrates | Protein |
|---|---|---|---|
| 301 | 18.1 grams | 1.3 grams | 30 grams |

## Leg of Lamb

| Yield | Preparation Time | Cooking Time |
|---|---|---|
| 10 servings | 15 minutes | 1 hour 25 minutes |

**Ingredients:**

- 1 (4 pound) grass-fed bone-in leg of lamb
- Salt and freshly ground black pepper, to taste
- 2 tablespoons butter
- 1 large yellow onion, sliced thinly
- 1 ½ cups homemade chicken broth, divided
- 2 tablespoons fresh lemon juice
- 6 garlic cloves, crushed
- 6 fresh thyme sprigs
- 3 fresh rosemary sprigs

**Directions:**

1. Season the leg of lamb with salt and black pepper generously.
2. Place the butter in the Instant Pot and select "Sauté." Then add the leg of lamb and sear for about 4 minutes per side or until browned completely.
3. Transfer the leg of lamb into a large plate.
4. Now add the onion and a little salt and cook for about 3 minutes.
5. Add a little broth and cook for about 2 minutes, scraping the brown bits from the bottom.
6. Select "Cancel" and stir in the cooked leg of lamb and remaining ingredients.
7. Secure the lid and place the pressure valve to the "Seal" position.
8. Select "Manual" and cook under "High Pressure" for about 75 minutes.
9. Select "Cancel" and carefully do a "Natural" release.
10. Remove the lid and with the tongs and transfer the leg of lamb onto a cutting board.
11. Strain the pan liquid into a bowl.
12. Cut the leg of lamb into desired-sized slices.
13. Pour in the strained liquid over the sliced leg of lamb and serve.

**Nutrition Information per Serving:**

| Calories | Fat | Carbohydrates | Protein |
| --- | --- | --- | --- |
| 455 | 33.1 grams | 2.6 grams | 33.2 grams |

## Lamb Shanks

| Yield | Preparation Time | Cooking Time |
|---|---|---|
| 4 servings | 10 minutes | 41 minutes |

**Ingredients:**

- 2 pounds grass-fed lamb shanks, trimmed
- **Salt and freshly ground black pepper,** to taste
- 3 tablespoons butter, divided
- 10 whole garlic cloves, peeled
- 1 cup homemade chicken broth
- 1 tablespoon sugar-free tomato paste
- ½ teaspoon crushed dried rosemary
- 2 tablespoons fresh lemon juice

**Directions:**

1. Season shanks with salt and pepper evenly.
2. Place two tablespoons of the butter in the Instant Pot and select "Sauté." Then add the shanks and sear for about 2-3 minutes per side or until browned completely.
3. Add the garlic cloves and cook for about 1 minute.
4. Select "Cancel" and stir in the remaining ingredients.
5. Secure the lid and place the pressure valve to the "Seal" position.
6. Select "Manual" and cook under "High Pressure" for about 30 minutes.
7. Select "Cancel" and carefully do a "Natural" release.
8. Remove the lid and with tongs and transfer the leg of lamb onto a platter.
9. Select "Sauté" and cook for about 5 minutes.
10. Stir in the lemon juice and remaining butter until smooth.
11. Pour in the sauce over the shanks and serve.

**Nutrition Information per Serving:**

| Calories | Fat | Carbohydrates | Protein |
|---|---|---|---|
| 525 | 25.7 grams | 3.7 grams | 60 grams |

## Lamb Curry

| Yield | Preparation Time | Cooking Time |
|---|---|---|
| 4 servings | 15 minutes | 35 minutes |

**Ingredients:**

- 1 pound grass-fed lamb shoulder, cut into bite-sized pieces
- 1 tablespoon curry powder, divided
- ¼ cup unsweetened coconut milk
- 4 tablespoons coconut cream
- 2 tablespoons coconut oil
- 1 medium yellow onion, chopped
- 1 teaspoon garlic paste
- 1 teaspoon ginger paste
- 1 teaspoon red chili powder
- ½ cup homemade chicken broth
- 1 tablespoon fresh lemon juice
- Salt and freshly ground black pepper, to taste
- 2 tablespoons chopped fresh cilantro

**Directions:**

1. In a large bowl, add the lamb, ½ tablespoon of curry powder, coconut milk, and coconut cream and mix well.
2. Set aside for at least 20 minutes.
3. After 20 minutes, remove the lamb from the bowl, reserving the cream mixture.
4. Place the oil in the Instant Pot and select "Sauté." Then add the onion, garlic, and ginger and cook for about 3-4 minutes.
5. Add the remaining curry powder and chili powder and cook for about 1 minute.
6. Add the lamb and cook for about 5 minutes.
7. Select "Cancel" and stir in the broth, lemon juice, salt, and black pepper.
8. Secure the lid and place the pressure valve to the "Seal" position.
9. Select "Manual" and cook under "High Pressure" for about 20 minutes.
10. Select "Cancel" and carefully do a "Quick" release.
11. Remove the lid and select "Sauté."
12. Stir in the reserved cream mixture and cook for about 4-5 minutes, stirring occasionally.
13. Serve immediately with the garnishing of cilantro.

**Nutrition Information per Serving:**

| Calories | Fat | Carbohydrates | Protein |
| --- | --- | --- | --- |
| 435 | 29.6 grams | 7 grams | 34.6 grams |

# Seafood Recipes

**Steamed Salmon**

| Yield | Preparation Time | Cooking Time |
|---|---|---|
| 4 servings | 10 minutes | 5 minutes |

**Ingredients:**

- 4 (6 ounce) salmon fillets
- ½ teaspoon red chili powder
- Salt and freshly ground black pepper, to taste
- ¼ cup fresh lemon juice
- 3 tablespoons unsalted butter, melted

**Directions:**

1. Arrange a trivet in the bottom of the Instant Pot and pour in ¾ cup of water and lemon juice.
2. Season the salmon fillets with chili powder, salt, and black pepper evenly.
3. Place the salmon fillets on top of the trivet in a single layer.
4. Secure the lid and place the pressure valve to the "Seal" position.
5. Select "Manual" and cook under "High Pressure" for about 5 minutes.
6. Select "Cancel" and carefully do a "Quick" release.
7. Remove the lid and transfer the salmon fillets onto serving plates.
8. Drizzle with the butter and serve immediately.

| Calories | Fat | Carbohydrates | Protein |
|---|---|---|---|
| 370 | 24 grams | 0.5 grams | 36 grams |

## Feta Salmon

| Yield | Preparation Time | Cooking Time |
|---|---|---|
| 4 servings | 10 minutes | 3 minutes |

- ¼ cup butter, melted
- 2 tablespoons fresh lemon juice
- 1 garlic clove, minced
- 1 tablespoon crumbled feta cheese
- ¼ teaspoon dried oregano
- Salt and freshly ground black pepper, to taste
- 1 pound salmon fillets
- 2 fresh rosemary sprigs
- 2 lemon slices

**Directions:**
1. In a large bowl, add the butter, lemon juice, garlic, feta, oregano, salt, and black pepper and beat until well combined.
2. Arrange the trivet in the bottom of the Instant Pot. Add 1 ½ cups of water in the Instant Pot.
3. Place the salmon fillets on top of a trivet in a single layer and top with dressing. Arrange one rosemary sprig and one lemon slice over each fillet.
4. Secure the lid and place the pressure valve to the "Seal" position.
5. Select "Steam" and just use the default time of 3 minutes.
6. Select "Cancel" and carefully do a "Quick" release.
7. Remove the lid and serve hot.

| Calories | Fat | Carbohydrates | Protein |
|---|---|---|---|
| 294 | 20.1 grams | 0.9 grams | 27.9 grams |

**Cod with Tomatoes**

| Yield | Preparation Time | Cooking Time |
|---|---|---|
| 4 servings | 15 minutes | 5 minutes |

**Ingredients:**

- ½ pound tomatoes, halved
- 2 tablespoons chopped fresh rosemary
- 4 (4 ounce) cod fillets
- 2 garlic cloves, minced
- 2 tablespoons butter, melted
- Salt and freshly ground black pepper, to taste

**Directions:**

1. In the bottom of a greased, large heatproof bowl, place half of the tomatoes, followed by the rosemary.
2. Arrange the cod fillets on top in a single layer, followed by the remaining tomatoes.
3. Sprinkle with garlic and drizzle with the melted butter.
4. Arrange the bowl in the bottom of the Instant Pot.
5. Secure the lid and place the pressure valve to the "Seal" position.
6. Select "Manual" and cook under "High Pressure" for about 5 minutes.
7. Select "Cancel" and carefully do a "Quick" release.
8. Remove the lid and transfer the fish fillets and tomatoes in serving plates.
9. Sprinkle with salt and black pepper and serve.

**Nutrition Information per Serving:**

| Calories | Fat | Carbohydrates | Protein |
| --- | --- | --- | --- |
| 294 | 20.1 grams | 0.9 grams | 27.9 grams |

## Fish Curry

| Yield | Preparation Time | Cooking Time |
|---|---|---|
| 6 servings | 15 minutes | 12 minutes |

**Ingredients:**

- 2 tablespoons coconut oil
- 2 curry leaves
- 1 yellow onion, chopped
- 1 tablespoon fresh ginger, grated finely
- 2 garlic cloves, minced
- 2 tablespoons curry powder
- 2 teaspoons ground cumin
- 2 teaspoons ground coriander
- 1 teaspoon red chili powder
- ½ teaspoon ground turmeric
- Salt, to taste
- 2 cups unsweetened coconut milk
- 1 ½ pounds white fish fillets, cubed
- 1 ¼ cups chopped tomatoes
- 1 Serrano pepper, seeded and chopped
- 1 tablespoon fresh lemon juice

**Directions:**

1. Place the oil in the Instant Pot and select "Sauté." Then add the curry leaves and cook for about 30 seconds.
2. Add the onion, ginger, and garlic and cook for about 4-5 minutes.
3. Add the spices and cook for about 1 ½ minutes.
4. Stir in the coconut milk.
5. Select "Cancel" and stir in the fish, tomatoes, and Serrano pepper.
6. Secure the lid and place the pressure valve to the "Seal" position.
7. Select "Manual" and cook under "Manual" and "Low Pressure" for about 5 minutes.
8. Select "Cancel" and carefully do a "Natural" release.
9. Remove the lid and stir in the lemon juice.
10. Serve hot.

**Nutrition Information per Serving:**

| Calories | Fat | Carbohydrates | Protein |
|---|---|---|---|
| 449 | 32.8 grams | 10 grams | 30.7 grams |

### Shrimp Curry

| Yield | Preparation Time | Cooking Time |
|---|---|---|
| 4 servings | 20 minutes | 13 minutes |

**Ingredients:**
- 1 tablespoon coconut oil
- 1 teaspoon mustard seeds
- 1 cup chopped yellow onion
- ½ tablespoon minced garlic
- ½ tablespoon minced fresh ginger
- 1 Serrano pepper, sliced
- 1 cup chopped tomatoes
- 1 ½ teaspoons red chili powder
- ½ teaspoon ground cumin
- ½ teaspoon ground coriander
- ½ teaspoon ground turmeric
- Salt, to taste
- 1 pound shrimp, peeled and deveined
- 3 ½ ounces unsweetened coconut milk
- 1 tablespoon fresh lemon juice
- ¼ cup chopped fresh cilantro

**Directions:**

1. Place the oil in the Instant Pot and select "Sauté." Then add the mustard seeds and cook for about 30 seconds.
2. Add the onion, garlic, ginger, and Serrano pepper and cook for about 4-5 minutes.
3. Add the tomato and spices and cook for about 2-3 minutes.
4. Select "Cancel" and stir in the shrimp and coconut milk.
5. Secure the lid and place the pressure valve to the "Seal" position.
6. Select "Manual" and cook under "Manual" and "Low Pressure" for about 3 minutes.
7. Select "Cancel" and carefully do a "Quick" release.
8. Remove the lid and stir in the lemon juice and cilantro.
9. Serve hot.

**Nutrition Information per Serving:**

| Calories | Fat | Carbohydrates | Protein |
|---|---|---|---|
| 263 | 12.4 grams | 11 grams | 28.1 grams |

## Creamy Shrimp

| Yield | Preparation Time | Cooking Time |
|---|---|---|
| 6 servings | 20 minutes | 20 minutes |

**Ingredients:**

**For Marinade:**

- ¼ cup plain yogurt
- 1 teaspoon grated fresh ginger
- 1 garlic clove, minced
- 2 teaspoons fresh lime juice
- 2 teaspoons garam masala powder
- 2 teaspoons ground cumin
- 2 teaspoons smoked paprika
- Salt, to taste
- 2 pounds large shrimp, peeled and deveined

**For Sauce:**

- 4 tablespoons unsalted butter, divided
- 1 small yellow onion, minced
- Salt, to taste
- 1 ½ teaspoons grated fresh ginger

- 2 garlic cloves, minced
- ½ teaspoon crushed red pepper flakes
- 1 (28 ounce) can sugar-free diced tomatoes with juice
- 1 cup heavy cream

**Directions:**

1. For the marinade: in a large bowl, add all of the ingredients except the shrimp and mix until well combined.
2. Add the shrimp and coat with marinade generously.
3. Refrigerate, covered, for about 1 hour.
4. For the sauce: place two tablespoons of butter in the Instant Pot and select "Sauté." Then add the onion and a pinch of salt and cook for about 4-5 minutes.
5. Stir in the ginger, garlic, red pepper flakes, and ¼ teaspoon of salt and cook for about 1-2 minutes.
6. Select "Cancel" and stir in the tomatoes and cream.
7. Secure the lid and place the pressure valve to the "Seal" position.
8. Select "Manual" and cook under "High Pressure" for about 8 minutes.
9. Select "Cancel" and carefully do a "Natural" release.
10. Remove the lid and select "Sauté."
11. Cook for about 3-5 minutes, stirring occasionally.
12. Stir in the shrimp with the liquid in the bowl and remaining butter and cook for about 3-4 minutes.
13. Select "Cancel" and serve hot.

**Nutrition Information per Serving:**

| Calories | Fat | Carbohydrates | Protein |
| --- | --- | --- | --- |
| 362 | 19 grams | 11 grams | 37 grams |

## Creamy Lobster

| Yield | Preparation Time | Cooking Time |
|---|---|---|
| 2 servings | 20 minutes | 3 minutes |

**Ingredients:**

- 1 ½ cups water
- 1 teaspoon old bay seasoning
- 2 pounds fresh lobster tails
- 1 scallion, chopped
- ½ cup mayonnaise
- 3 tablespoons unsalted butter, melted
- 2 tablespoons fresh lemon juice, divided

**Directions:**

1. Arrange a steamer trivet in the bottom of the Instant Pot and pour in the water and 1-2 pinches of old bay seasoning.
2. Arrange the lobster tails on top of the trivet, shell side down.
3. Drizzle the lobster tails with one tablespoon of lemon juice.
4. Secure the lid and place the pressure valve to the "Seal" position.
5. Select "Manual" and cook under "High Pressure" for about 3 minutes.
6. Select "Cancel" and carefully do a "Quick" release.

7. Remove the lid and transfer the tails into the bowl of the ice bath for about 1 minute.
8. With kitchen shears, cut the underbelly of the tail down the center.
9. Remove the meat and chop it up into large chunks.
10. In a large bowl, add the scallions, mayonnaise, butter, seasoning, and lemon juice and mix well.
11. Transfer the lobster meat onto a platter and top with the sauce.
12. Refrigerate for at least 15 minutes before serving.

**Nutrition Information per Serving:**

| Calories | Fat | Carbohydrates | Protein |
|---|---|---|---|
| 495 | 25 grams | 10 grams | 58.1 grams |

## Lemony Mussels

| Yield | Preparation Time | Cooking Time |
|---|---|---|
| 4 servings | 15 minutes | 7 minutes |

**Ingredients:**

- 2 tablespoons butter
- 1 medium yellow onion, chopped
- 1 garlic clove, minced
- ½ teaspoon crushed dried rosemary
- 1 cup homemade chicken broth
- 2 tablespoons fresh lemon juice
- Salt and freshly ground black pepper, to taste
- 2 pounds mussels, cleaned and de-bearded

**Instructions:**

1. Place the butter in the Instant Pot and select "Sauté." Then add the onion and cook for about 5 minutes.
2. Add the garlic and rosemary and cook for about 1 minute.
3. Select "Cancel" and stir in the broth, lemon juice, and black pepper.
4. Place the mussels in the steamer trivet and arrange the trivet in the Instant Pot.
5. Secure the lid and place the pressure valve to the "Seal" position.
6. Select "Manual" and cook under "Low Pressure" for about 1 minute.
7. Select "Cancel" and carefully do a "Quick" release.
8. Remove the lid and transfer the mussels into a serving bowl.
9. Top with the cooking liquid and serve.

**Nutrition Information per Serving:**

| Calories | Fat | Carbohydrates | Protein |
|---|---|---|---|
| 270 | 12 grams | 11 grams | 28.6 grams |

## Mussels in Tomato Gravy

| Yield | Preparation Time | Cooking Time |
|---|---|---|
| 4 servings | 15 minutes | 3 minutes |

**Ingredients:**

- 2 large Roma tomatoes, seeded and chopped finely
- 2 garlic cloves, minced
- 1 cup homemade chicken broth
- 1 tablespoon fresh lemon juice
- 2 pounds mussels, scrubbed and de-bearded

**Instructions:**

1. In the pot of the Instant Pot, place the tomatoes, garlic, wine, and bay leaf and stir to combine.
2. Arrange the mussels on top.
3. Secure the lid and place the pressure valve to the "Seal" position.
4. Select "Manual" and cook under "High Pressure" for about 3 minutes.
5. Select "Cancel" and carefully do a "Quick" release.
6. Remove the lid and serve hot.

| Calories | Fat | Carbohydrates | Protein |
|---|---|---|---|
| 219 | 5.6 grams | 11 grams | 28.9 grams |

## Buttered Crab Legs

| Yield | Preparation Time | Cooking Time |
|---|---|---|
| 2 servings | 20 minutes | 4 minutes |

**Ingredients:**

- 1 ½ pounds frozen crab legs
- Salt, to taste
- 2 tablespoons butter, melted

**Directions:**

1. Arrange a trivet in the bottom of the Instant Pot and pour in one cup of water with one teaspoon of salt.
2. Place the crab legs on top of the trivet and sprinkle with salt.
3. Secure the lid and place the pressure valve to the "Seal" position.
4. Select "Manual" and cook under "High Pressure" for about 4 minutes.
5. Select "Cancel" and carefully do a "Quick" release.
6. Remove the lid and transfer the crab legs onto a serving platter.
7. Drizzle with butter and serve.

**Nutrition Information per Serving:**

| Calories | Fat | Carbohydrates | Protein |
|---|---|---|---|
| 297 | 11.1 grams | 0 grams | 43.6 grams |

# Vegetarian Recipes

## Beet Salad

| Yield | Preparation Time | Cooking Time |
|---|---|---|
| 7 servings | 15 minutes | 24 minutes |

- 1 ¾ pounds medium beets, trimmed
- 2 tablespoons butter, melted
- Salt and freshly ground black pepper, to taste
- 8 cups fresh baby spinach
- 2 tablespoons crumbled feta cheese

**Directions:**
1. Arrange a steamer basket in the bottom of the Instant Pot and pour in one cup of water.
2. Place the beets in the steamer basket.
3. Secure the lid and place the pressure valve to the "Seal" position.
4. Select "Manual" and cook under "High Pressure" for about 24 minutes.
5. Select "Cancel" and carefully do a "Quick" release.
6. Remove the lid and transfer the beets onto a cutting board to cool slightly.
7. Carefully, remove the peel of the beets and cut into wedges.
8. In a bowl, add the beets, butter, salt, and black pepper and gently toss to coat.
9. Divide the spinach onto serving plates and top with beet wedges.
10. Garnish with feta and serve.

| Calories | Fat | Carbohydrates | Protein |
|---|---|---|---|
| 94 | 4.2 grams | 12 grams | 3.3 grams |

## Creamy Cauliflower Rice

| Yield | Preparation Time | Cooking Time |
|---|---|---|
| 4 servings | 15 minutes | 8 minutes |

- 2 cups grated into rice consistency cauliflower
- ½ cup shredded sharp cheddar cheese
- ½ cup half-and-half
- 2 tablespoons cream cheese, softened
- Salt and freshly ground black pepper, to taste

**Directions:**
1. In the bottom of the Instant Pot, arrange a steamer trivet and pour in 1 ½ cups of water.
2. In a heatproof bowl that will fit in an Instant Pot, add all ingredients and stir to combine.
3. With a piece of foil, cover the bowl.
4. Place the bowl on top of the trivet.
5. Secure the lid and place the pressure valve to the "Seal" position.
6. Select "Manual" and cook under "Low Pressure" for about 5 minutes.
7. Meanwhile, preheat the oven to broil.
8. Select "Cancel" and carefully do a "Natural" release for about 10 minutes, and then do a "Quick" release.
9. Remove the lid and transfer the bowl onto a counter.
10. Remove the foil and broil for about 2-3 minutes.
11. Remove from oven and serve hot.

**Nutritional Information per Serving**

| Calories | Fat | Carbohydrates | Protein |
|---|---|---|---|
| 126 | 10 grams | 4.3 grams | 5.8 grams |

## Cheesy Zucchini Noodles

| Yield | Preparation Time | Cooking Time |
|---|---|---|
| 3 servings | 15 minutes | 2 minutes |

**Ingredients:**

- 2 tablespoons olive oil
- 2 garlic cloves, chopped finely
- 2 large zucchinis, spiralized with blade C
- 4 tablespoons grated Parmesan cheese
- Salt and freshly ground black pepper, to taste

**Directions:**

1. Place the oil in the Instant Pot and select "Sauté." Then add the garlic and sauté for about 30 seconds.
2. Add the zucchini noodles and sauté for about 30-40 seconds.
3. Add the Parmesan and gently stir to combine.
4. Select "Cancel" and serve immediately.

| Calories | Fat | Carbohydrates | Protein |
|---|---|---|---|
| 93 | 7.6 grams | 5.9 grams | 2 grams |

## Buttered Asparagus

| Yield | Preparation Time | Cooking Time |
|---|---|---|
| 4 servings | 15 minutes | 8 minutes |

**Ingredients:**
- 1 pound fresh asparagus, trimmed
- 3 garlic cloves, minced
- 3 tablespoons butter
- Salt and freshly ground black pepper, to taste

**Directions:**
1. Place asparagus in the center of a foil piece with garlic and butter.
2. Curve the edges of foil to prevent the butter running off.
3. In the pot of the Instant Pot, place one cup of water.
4. Carefully place the foil in the pot.
5. Secure the lid and place the pressure valve to the "Seal" position.
6. Select "Manual" and cook under "High Pressure" for about 8 minutes.
7. Select "Cancel" and carefully do a "Quick" release.
8. Remove the lid and transfer the asparagus onto serving plates.
9. Sprinkle with salt and black pepper and serve.

| Calories | Fat | Carbohydrates | Protein |
|---|---|---|---|
| 102 | 8.8 grams | 5.2 grams | 2.7 grams |

## Buttered Brussels Sprout

| Yield | Preparation Time | Cooking Time |
|---|---|---|
| 4 servings | 15 minutes | 3 minutes |

### Ingredients:

- 1 pound Brussels sprouts, trimmed and halved
- 2 tablespoons unsalted butter, melted
- Salt and freshly ground black pepper, to taste

### Directions:

1. Arrange a steamer trivet in the bottom of the Instant Pot and pour in one cup of water.
2. Place the Brussels sprouts in the trivet.
3. Secure the lid and place the pressure valve to the "Seal" position.
4. Select "Manual" and cook under "High Pressure" for about 3 minutes.
5. Select "Cancel" and carefully do a "Quick" release.
6. Remove the lid and transfer the Brussels sprouts onto serving plates.
7. Drizzle with the melted butter and sprinkle with salt and black pepper
8. Serve immediately.

| Calories | Fat | Carbohydrates | Protein |
|---|---|---|---|
| 100 | 6.2 grams | 10.3 grams | 3.9 grams |

## Garlicky Broccoli

| Yield | Preparation Time | Cooking Time |
|---|---|---|
| 4 servings | 10 minutes | 5 minutes |

**Ingredients:**
- 1 pound broccoli florets
- 2 tablespoons butter, melted
- 3 garlic cloves, chopped
- 1 jalapeño pepper, chopped finely
- ¼ teaspoon crushed red pepper flakes
- Salt and freshly ground black pepper, to taste

**Directions:**
1. Arrange a trivet in the bottom of the Instant Pot and pour in one cup of water.
2. Place the broccoli florets on top of trivet in a single layer.
3. Secure the lid and place the pressure valve to the "Seal" position.
4. Select "Manual" and cook under "High Pressure" for about 3-5 minutes.
5. Select "Cancel" and carefully do a "Quick" release.
6. Meanwhile, in a frying pan, melt the butter over medium heat and sauté the garlic, jalapeño, and red pepper flakes for about 1 minute.
7. Stir in salt and black pepper and remove from the heat.
8. Remove the lid and transfer the broccoli onto a serving platter.
9. Drizzle with garlic mixture and serve immediately.

| Calories | Fat | Carbohydrates | Protein |
|---|---|---|---|
| 94 | 6.2 grams | 8.5 grams | 3.4 grams |

## Feta Green Beans

| Yield | Preparation Time | Cooking Time |
|---|---|---|
| 4 servings | 15 minutes | 5 minutes |

**Ingredients:**
- 1 pound fresh green beans
- 2 tablespoons butter
- 2 garlic cloves, minced
- Salt and freshly ground black pepper, to taste
- 1½ cups water
- ¼ cup crumbled feta cheese
- 2 tablespoons chopped walnuts

**Directions:**
1. In the pot of the Instant Pot, add all of the ingredients and stir to combine.
2. Secure the lid and place the pressure valve to the "Seal" position.
3. Select "Manual" and cook under "High Pressure" for about 5 minutes.
4. Select "Cancel" and carefully do a "Quick" release.
5. Remove the lid and transfer onto a platter.
6. Serve warm with the topping of feta and walnuts.

| Calories | Fat | Carbohydrates | Protein |
|---|---|---|---|
| 137 | 10.2 grams | 9.4 grams | 4.5 grams |

## Cheesy Cauliflower

| Yield | Preparation Time | Cooking Time |
|---|---|---|
| 4 servings | 15 minutes | 14 minutes |

**Ingredients:**

**For Sauce:**

- 6 ounces goat cheese
- 1/3 cup heavy cream
- 1 tablespoon olive oil
- 1 teaspoon ground nutmeg
- Salt and ground white pepper, to taste

**For Cauliflower:**

- 1 (2 pound) head cauliflower
- 1 cup homemade vegetable broth
- 2 tablespoons fresh lemon juice
- 2 tablespoons olive oil
- 2 teaspoons crushed red pepper flakes
- Salt to taste

**Directions:**

1. For the sauce: in a food processor, add all of the ingredients and pulse until smooth. Keep aside until serving.
2. In the pot of the Instant Pot, place the cauliflower head and top with the remaining ingredients.
3. Secure the lid and place the pressure valve to the "Seal" position.
4. Select "Manual" and cook under "High Pressure" for about 10 minutes.
5. Meanwhile, preheat the oven to broil.
6. Select "Cancel" and carefully do a "Quick" release.
7. Remove the lid and transfer the cauliflower head onto a cutting board.
8. Cut the cauliflower head into pieces and place onto a broiler pan.
9. Broil for about 3-4 minutes or until golden brown.
10. Remove from oven and serve with the topping of cheese sauce.

**Nutrition Information per Serving:**

| Calories | Fat | Carbohydrates | Protein |
|---|---|---|---|
| 312 | 24.3 grams | 11 grams | 15.3 grams |

## Creamy Mushrooms

| Yield | Preparation Time | Cooking Time |
|---|---|---|
| 5 servings | 15 minutes | 4 minutes |

### Ingredients:

- 1 ½ pounds cremini mushrooms
- 4 garlic cloves, chopped finely
- ¼ teaspoon dried thyme
- ½ teaspoon dried oregano
- ½ teaspoon dried basil
- 2 bay leaves
- 1 cup homemade vegetable broth
- Salt and freshly ground black pepper, to taste
- ¼ cup half-and-half
- 2 tablespoons unsalted butter
- 2 tablespoons chopped fresh parsley leaves

**Directions:**

1. In the pot of the Instant Pot, add all of the ingredients except the half-and-half, butter, and parsley and stir to combine.
2. Secure the lid and place the pressure valve to the "Seal" position.
3. Select "Manual" and cook under "High Pressure" for about 4 minutes.
4. Select "Cancel" and carefully do a "Quick" release.
5. Remove the lid and stir in the half-and-half, butter, and parsley.
6. Serve warm.

**Nutrition Information per Serving:**

| Calories | Fat | Carbohydrates | Protein |
|---|---|---|---|
| 154 | 9.9 grams | 8.4 grams | 6.2 grams |

## Spinach with Cottage Cheese

| Yield | Preparation Time | Cooking Time |
|---|---|---|
| 4 servings | 15 minutes | 10 minutes |

**Ingredients:**

- 2 tablespoons butter
- 1 small yellow onion, chopped
- 4 garlic cloves, chopped
- 1 Serrano pepper, chopped
- ½ teaspoon ground cumin
- ¼ teaspoon ground coriander
- 1 tomato, chopped
- 10 ounces fresh spinach
- Salt and freshly ground black pepper, to taste
- 10 ounces cottage cheese, cubed

**Directions:**

1. Place the butter in the Instant Pot and select "Sauté." Then add the onion, garlic, Serrano, and spices and cook for about 3-4 minutes.
2. Add the tomato and cook for about 2 minutes.
3. Select "Cancel" and stir in spinach, salt, and black pepper.
4. Secure the lid and place the pressure valve to the "Seal" position.
5. Select "Manual" and cook under "High Pressure" for about 2 minutes.
6. Select "Cancel" and carefully do a "Natural" release.
7. Remove the lid and with an immersion blender puree the spinach mixture.
8. Select the "Sauté" and stir in cottage cheese.
9. Cook for about 2 minutes.
10. Select "Cancel" and serve.

**Nutrition Information per Serving:**

| Calories | Fat | Carbohydrates | Protein |
|---|---|---|---|
| 147 | 7.6 grams | 8.6 grams | 12 grams |

**Spiced Kale**

| Yield | Preparation Time | Cooking Time |
|---|---|---|
| 3 servings | 10 minutes | 5 minutes |

**Ingredients:**

- 2 tablespoons butter
- 1 teaspoon cumin seeds
- 2 garlic cloves, chopped finely
- ½ teaspoon red chili powder
- ¼ teaspoon ground turmeric
- Salt, to taste
- 1 (10 ounce) package fresh baby kale
- 2 tablespoons water

**Directions:**

1. Place the butter in the Instant Pot and select "Sauté." Then add the cumin seeds and sauté for about 30 seconds.
2. Add the garlic and sauté for about 30 seconds.
3. Select "Cancel" and stir in the kale, chili powder, turmeric, and salt.
4. Secure the lid and place the pressure valve to the "Seal" position.
5. Select "Steam" and just use the default time of 1 minute.
6. Select "Cancel" and carefully do a "Quick" release.
7. Remove the lid and select "Sauté."
8. Cook for about 2-3 minutes.
9. Select "Cancel" and serve hot.

**Nutrition Information per Serving:**

| Calories | Fat | Carbohydrates | Protein |
|---|---|---|---|
| 122 | 7.9 grams | 11 grams | 3.2 grams |

## Zucchini with Tomatoes

| Yield | Preparation Time | Cooking Time |
|---|---|---|
| 8 servings | 15 minutes | 7 minutes |

**Ingredients:**
- 2 tablespoons butter
- 1 small yellow onion, chopped roughly
- 2 garlic cloves, minced
- 6 medium zucchinis, chopped roughly
- 1 pound cherry tomatoes
- 1 cup water
- Salt and freshly ground black pepper, to taste
- 2 tablespoons chopped fresh basil

**Directions:**
1. Place the oil in the Instant Pot and select "Sauté." Then add the onion and garlic and cook for about 3-4 minutes.
2. Add zucchinis and tomatoes and cook for about 1-2 minutes.
3. Select "Cancel" and stir in remaining ingredients except the basil.
4. Secure the lid and place the pressure valve to the "Seal" position.
5. Select "Manual" and cook under "High Pressure" for about 5 minutes.
6. Select "Cancel" and carefully do a "Natural" release.
7. Remove the lid and serve hot.

| Calories | Fat | Carbohydrates | Protein |
|---|---|---|---|
| 85 | 4.4 grams | 11 grams | 3.3 grams |

## Mixed Greens Curry

| Yield | Preparation Time | Cooking Time |
|---|---|---|
| 6 servings | 15 minutes | 9 minutes |

**Ingredients:**

- 3 tablespoons butter
- 1 medium yellow onion, chopped
- 4 garlic cloves, minced
- 1 (2-inch) piece fresh ginger, minced
- 1 teaspoon garam masala
- 1 teaspoon ground cumin
- 1 teaspoon ground coriander
- ½ teaspoon red chili powder
- ½ teaspoon ground turmeric
- Salt and black pepper, to taste
- 1 pound mustard leaves, rinsed
- 1 pound fresh spinach, rinsed
- 1/3 cup heavy cream

**Directions:**

1. Place the butter in the Instant Pot and select "Sauté." Then add the onion, garlic, ginger, and spices and cook for about 2-3 minutes.
2. Add greens and cook for about 2 minutes.
3. Select "Cancel" and stir well.
4. Secure the lid and place the pressure valve to the "Seal" position.
5. Select "Manual" and cook under "High Pressure" for about 4 minutes.
6. Select "Cancel" and carefully do a "Natural" release.
7. Remove the lid and stir in the cream.
8. With an immersion blender, blend the mixture until smooth.
9. Serve immediately.

**Nutrition Information per Serving:**

| Calories | Fat | Carbohydrates | Protein |
|---|---|---|---|
| 125 | 8.9 grams | 9 grams | 4.9 grams |

## Eggplant Curry

| Yield | Preparation Time | Cooking Time |
|---|---|---|
| 4 servings | 15 minutes | 17 minutes |

**Ingredients:**

- ¼ cup coconut oil
- 1 large eggplant, chopped
- ½ yellow onion, chopped
- 3 garlic cloves, minced
- 1/3 cup chopped tomato
- ¼ teaspoon ground cumin
- ¼ teaspoon cayenne pepper
- ¼ teaspoon ground turmeric
- ½ cup water
- 2 tablespoons chopped fresh cilantro

**Instructions:**

1. Place two tablespoons of oil in the Instant Pot and select "Sauté." Then add half of the eggplant slices and cook for about 5 minutes.
2. Transfer the eggplant slices into a bowl.
3. Repeat with two more tablespoons of oil and remaining eggplant slices.
4. Add remaining oil, cooked eggplant slices, onion, and garlic and cook for about 1-2 minutes.
5. Select "Cancel" and stir in the remaining ingredients except the cilantro.
6. Secure the lid and place the pressure valve to the "Seal" position.
7. Select "Manual" and cook under "High Pressure" for about 3 minutes.
8. Select "Cancel" and carefully do a "Quick" release.
9. Remove the lid and select "Sauté."
10. Cook for about 1-2 minutes.
11. Select "Cancel" and remove the lid.
12. Serve hot.

**Nutrition Information per Serving:**

| Calories | Fat | Carbohydrates | Protein |
|---|---|---|---|
| 159 | 14 grams | 9.6 grams | 1.6 grams |

## Mixed Veggies

| Yield | Preparation Time | Cooking Time |
|---|---|---|
| 5 servings | 20 minutes | 7 minutes |

### Ingredients:

- 1 large zucchini, sliced into thin circles
- 1 large eggplant, sliced into thin circles
- 2 medium tomatoes, sliced into thin circles
- 1 small yellow onion, sliced into thin circles
- 1 tablespoon minced fresh thyme leaves, divided
- Salt and freshly ground black pepper, to taste
- 2 large garlic cloves, chopped finely
- 2 tablespoons butter, melted
- 1 tablespoon fresh lemon juice

**Directions:**

1. In the bottom of the Instant Pot, arrange a steamer trivet and pour in one cup of water.
2. In a bowl, add all vegetables, half of the thyme, salt, and black pepper and toss to coat well.
3. In the bottom of a foil-lined spring form, spread some of the garlic.
4. Arrange alternating slices of zucchini, eggplant, tomatoes, and onion, starting at the outer edge of the pan towards the center, overlapping the slices slightly.
5. Sprinkle with the remaining garlic, thyme, salt, and black pepper.
6. Drizzle with the melted butter and lemon juice evenly.
7. Place the spring form pan on top of the trivet.
8. Secure the lid and place the pressure valve to the "Seal" position.
9. Select "Manual" and cook under "High Pressure" for about 6 minutes.
10. Select "Cancel" and carefully do a "Natural" release for about 5 minutes. Then do a "Quick" release.
11. Remove the lid and serve hot.

**Nutrition Information per Serving:**

| Calories | Fat | Carbohydrates | Protein |
|----------|-----------|---------------|-----------|
| 92 | 6.1 grams | 11.2 grams | 2.4 grams |

# Poultry Recipes

### Roasted Cornish Hens

| Yield | Preparation Time | Cooking Time |
|---|---|---|
| 4 servings | 20 minutes | 23 minutes |

**Ingredients:**

- 2 Cornish hens, washed and patted dried
- Salt and freshly ground black pepper, to taste
- 2 tablespoons coconut oil
- 1 small yellow onion, chopped
- 2 celery stalks, chopped
- 1 large carrot, peeled and chopped
- 4 garlic cloves, chopped
- 2 teaspoons Worcestershire sauce
- 1 cup water

**Directions:**

1. Season the hens with salt and black pepper generously.
2. Place the oil in the Instant Pot and select "Sauté." Then add the hens, one at a time, and cook for about 2 minutes per side.
3. Select "Cancel" and arrange both hens in the Instant Pot. Top with the remaining ingredients.
4. Secure the lid and place the pressure valve to the "Seal" position.
5. Select "Manual" and cook under "Medium-High Pressure" for about 15 minutes.
6. Select "Cancel" and carefully do a "Natural" release.
7. Remove the lid and transfer the hens onto a platter for about 5 minutes before serving.

**Nutrition Information per Serving:**

| Calories | Fat | Carbohydrates | Protein |
|---|---|---|---|
| 249 | 11.7 grams | 5.2 grams | 29.7 grams |

## Roasted Chicken

| Yield | Preparation Time | Cooking Time |
|---|---|---|
| 4 servings | 15 minutes | 31 minutes |

**Ingredients:**

- 1 (2 ½-pound) grass-fed whole chicken, neck, and giblet removed
- 1 tablespoon cayenne pepper
- Salt and freshly ground black pepper, to taste
- 3 tablespoons butter
- 1 ½ cups homemade chicken broth

**Directions:**

1. Season the chicken with cayenne pepper, salt, and black pepper generously.
2. Place the butter in the Instant Pot and select "Sauté." Then add the chicken and cook for about 5-6 minute or until browned.
3. Select "Cancel" and transfer the chicken onto a plate.

4. Arrange a trivet in the bottom of the Instant Pot and pour in the chicken broth into the Instant Pot.
5. Arrange the chicken on top of the trivet, breast side up.
6. Secure the lid and place the pressure valve to the "Seal" position.
7. Select "Manual" and cook under "High Pressure" for about 25 minutes.
8. Select "Cancel" and carefully do a "Natural" release.
9. Remove the lid and place chicken onto a cutting board for about 10 minutes before carving.
10. With a sharp knife, cut the chicken into desires-sized pieces and serve.

**Nutrition Information per Serving:**

| Calories | Fat | Carbohydrates | Protein |
|---|---|---|---|
| 523 | 18 grams | 1.1 grams | 84.1 grams |

**Stuffed Chicken Breast**

| Yield | Preparation Time | Cooking Time |
|---|---|---|
| 4 servings | 20 minutes | 25 minutes |

**Ingredients:**

- 2 (6 ounce) grass-fed boneless, skinless chicken breasts
- Salt and freshly ground black pepper, to taste
- 4 thin prosciutto slices
- 4 thin provolone cheese slices
- 16 fresh basil leaves
- 1 tablespoon olive oil
- 3 tablespoons butter, divided
- 2 cups homemade chicken broth, divided
- 1 teaspoon balsamic vinegar
- 2 tablespoons minced fresh parsley

**Directions:**

1. Butterfly each chicken breast horizontally then carefully open each one in half.
2. With a meat mallet, pound each breast into ¼-inch thickness.
3. Season each chicken breast with salt and pepper evenly.
4. Arrange chicken breasts onto a smooth surface, cut side up.

5. Place two prosciutto slices in each chicken breast, followed by two provolone cheese slices and eight basil leaves.
6. Roll each chicken breast lengthwise and with kitchen twine and tie together.
7. Place the oil and one tablespoon of butter in the Instant Pot and select "Sauté." Then add the chicken rolls and sear for about 2 minutes per side.
8. Select "Cancel" and transfer chicken rolls onto a plate.
9. In the bottom of the Instant Pot, arrange a steamer trivet and pour in one cup of broth.
10. Place the chicken rolls on top of the trivet.
11. Secure the lid and place the pressure valve to the "Seal" position.
12. Select "Poultry" and just use the default time of 8 minutes.
13. Select "Cancel" and carefully do a "Natural" release for about 5 minutes and then do a "Quick" release.
14. Remove the lid and transfer the chicken onto a plate for about 5-10 minutes.
15. Remove the trivet from the Instant Pot and drain the broth. With paper towels, pat dry the pot.
16. Place one tablespoon of butter in the Instant Pot and select "Sauté." Then add the onion and cook for about 4-5 minutes, flipping once halfway through.
17. Add the remaining broth, vinegar, salt, and black pepper and simmer for about 3-5 minutes or until desired thickness of sauce.
18. Add remaining butter and parsley and stir to combine.
19. Meanwhile, cut each chicken roll into ½-inch slices.
20. Select "Cancel" and pour in the sauce over chicken slices.
21. Serve immediately.

**Nutrition Information per Serving:**

| Calories | Fat | Carbohydrates | Protein |
|---|---|---|---|
| 294 | 23 grams | 1.7 grams | 20 grams |

## BBQ Chicken Thighs

| Yield | Preparation Time | Cooking Time |
|---|---|---|
| 8 servings | 15 minutes | 18 minutes |

### Ingredients:

- ½ cup sugar-free BBQ sauce
- ½ cup water
- 2 tablespoons fresh lemon juice
- 3 tablespoons butter
- 2 pounds grass-fed boneless, skinless chicken thighs
- 1 teaspoon crushed red pepper flakes
- Salt and freshly ground black pepper, to taste
- 1 yellow onion, minced

**Directions:**

1. In a bowl, mix together the BBQ sauce, water, and lemon juice. Set aside.
2. Place the butter in the Instant Pot and select "Sauté." Then add the chicken thighs and cook for about 2 minutes per side.
3. Stir in the paprika, salt, and black pepper and cook for about 1 minute.
4. Select "Cancel" and stir in the BBQ sauce mixture.
5. Secure the lid and place the pressure valve to the "Seal" position.
6. Select "Manual" and cook under "High Pressure" for about 15 minutes.
7. Select "Cancel" and carefully do a "Natural" release.
8. Remove the lid and serve hot.

**Nutrition Information per Serving:**

| Calories | Fat | Carbohydrates | Protein |
|---|---|---|---|
| 272 | 12 grams | 7.2 grams | 33 grams |

## Chicken Legs

| Yield | Preparation Time | Cooking Time |
|---|---|---|
| 4 servings | 15 minutes | 20 minutes |

**Ingredients:**

- 1 cup homemade chicken broth
- 4 (8 ounce) grass-fed skinless chicken leg quarters
- 1 teaspoon garlic powder
- Salt and freshly ground black pepper, to taste
- 2 tablespoons butter, melted

**Directions:**

1. Arrange a trivet in the bottom of the Instant Pot. Add the broth into the Instant Pot.
2. Season the chicken leg quarters with garlic powder, salt, and black pepper.
3. Place the chicken leg quarters on top of the trivet in a single layer.
4. Secure the lid and place the pressure valve to the "Seal" position.

5. Select "Manual" and cook under "High Pressure" for about 20 minutes.
6. Meanwhile, preheat the oven to broil.
7. Select "Cancel" and carefully do a "Quick" release.
8. Remove the lid and with tongs transfer the chicken leg quarters onto a parchment paper lined baking sheet.
9. Coat the chicken leg quarters with the melted butter evenly and broil for about 5 minutes per side.
10. Serve hot.

**Nutrition Information per Serving:**

| Calories | Fat | Carbohydrates | Protein |
| --- | --- | --- | --- |
| 457 | 34 grams | 0.8 grams | 39.8 grams |

## Butter Chicken

| Yield | Preparation Time | Cooking Time |
|---|---|---|
| 8 servings | 15 minutes | 15 minutes |

**Ingredients:**

- 2 (14 ounce) cans diced tomatoes with liquid
- 1 tablespoon chopped garlic
- 2 jalapeño peppers, seeded and chopped
- ½ cup butter
- 10 (4 ounce) grass-fed skinless, boneless chicken thighs, cubed
- 1 tablespoon paprika
- ¼ teaspoon cayenne pepper
- 2 teaspoons ground cumin
- 1 teaspoon ground coriander
- ½ teaspoon ground turmeric
- ¾ cup plain Greek yogurt, whipped
- 1 cup heavy cream
- Salt, to taste
- 2 tablespoons arrowroot starch
- 2 tablespoons water
- ¼ cup chopped fresh cilantro

**Directions:**

1. In a food processor, add the canned tomatoes, garlic, and jalapeño peppers and pulse until smooth. Set aside.
2. Place the butter in the Instant Pot and select "Sauté." Then add the chicken pieces and cook for about 5 minutes or until browned. Transfer the chicken into a bowl.
3. In the pot, add the spices and cook for about 1 minute.
4. Select "Cancel" and stir in the cooked chicken, yogurt, cream, tomato mixture, and salt.
5. Secure the lid and place the pressure valve to the "Seal" position.
6. Select "Manual" and cook under "High Pressure" for about 5 minutes.
7. Select "Cancel" and carefully do a "Natural" release.
8. Meanwhile, in a small bowl, dissolve arrowroot starch in water.
9. Remove the lid and select "Sauté."
10. Add arrowroot starch mixture, stirring continuously, and cook for about 3-4 minutes.
11. Select "Cancel" and serve hot with the garnishing of cilantro.

**Nutrition Information per Serving:**

| Calories | Fat | Carbohydrates | Protein |
|---|---|---|---|
| 380 | 22.9 grams | 9 grams | 34.6 grams |

## Chicken Curry

| Yield | Preparation Time | Cooking Time |
|---|---|---|
| 6 servings | 15 minutes | 18 minutes |

**Ingredients:**

- 1 ½ pounds grass-fed boneless, skinless chicken breasts
- 3 garlic cloves, crushed
- 1 ½ tablespoons curry powder
- 1 teaspoon ground turmeric
- 1 (14 ounce) can diced tomatoes
- Salt and freshly ground black pepper, to taste
- 1 (14 ounce) cans full-fat coconut milk
- 6 ounces coconut cream
- 2 tablespoons coconut oil
- 2 tablespoons chopped fresh cilantro

**Directions:**

1. In the pot of the Instant Pot, add all of the ingredients except the coconut cream and coconut oil and stir to combine.
2. Secure the lid and place the pressure valve to the "Seal" position.
3. Select "Manual" and cook under "High Pressure" for about 8 minutes.
4. Select "Cancel" and carefully do a "Natural" release for about 10 minutes, and then do a "Quick" release.
5. Remove the lid and select "Sauté."
6. Stir in the coconut cream and coconut oil and cook for about 10 minutes.
7. Select "Cancel" and with a slotted spoon transfer the chicken breasts onto a cutting board.
8. Cut the chicken breasts into desired-sized pieces.
9. Return the chicken into the sauce and stir to combine.
10. Serve immediately with the garnishing of cilantro.

**Nutrition Information per Serving:**

| Calories | Fat | Carbohydrates | Protein |
| --- | --- | --- | --- |
| 569 | 43.8 grams | 10 grams | 36.7 grams |

## Cheesy Chicken

| Yield | Preparation Time | Cooking Time |
|---|---|---|
| 4 servings | 15 minutes | 14 minutes |

**Ingredients:**

- 2 tablespoons butter
- 4 (6 ounce) grass-fed skinless, boneless frozen chicken breasts
- 1 cup tomato sauce
- 1 cup mild salsa
- 3 tablespoons fresh lime juice
- Salt and ground black pepper, to taste
- 1 ½ cups grated mozzarella cheese

**Directions:**

1. Place the butter in the Instant Pot and select "Sauté." Then add the chicken and cook for about 5 minutes or until browned completely.
2. Add the remaining ingredients except the cheese and stir to combine.
3. Secure the lid and place the pressure valve to the "Seal" position.
4. Select "Manual" and cook under "High Pressure" for about 12 minutes.
5. Meanwhile, preheat the oven to broil. Grease a baking dish.
6. Select "Cancel" and carefully do a "Quick" release.
7. Remove the lid and with tongs transfer the chicken breasts into a prepared baking dish.
8. Now, select "Sauté" and cook the salsa mixture for about 2-3 minutes or until desired thickness is reached.
9. Pour in the sauce over the chicken thighs and sprinkle with cheese.
10. Broil for about 4-5 minutes.
11. Serve hot.

**Nutrition Information per Serving:**

| Calories | Fat | Carbohydrates | Protein |
|---|---|---|---|
| 421 | 21.5 grams | 7 grams | 48 grams |

## Roasted Duck

| Yield | Preparation Time | Cooking Time |
|---|---|---|
| 4 servings | 15 minutes | 43 minutes |

**Ingredients:**

- 1 (3 ½ pound) wild duck
- Salt and freshly ground black pepper, to taste
- 1 lemon, halved
- 2 sprigs fresh rosemary
- 3 tablespoons butter
- ½ cup homemade chicken broth

**Directions:**

1. With a fork, prick the skin of the duck.
2. Season the body and cavity of duck with salt and black pepper evenly.
3. Stuff the cavity of duck with lemon halves and rosemary sprigs and tie up the legs together.
4. Place the butter in the Instant Pot and select "Sauté." Then add the duck and cook for about 4-5 minutes or until browned from all sides.
5. Select "Cancel" and remove the grease from the pot.

6. Add the broth into the Instant Pot.
7. Secure the lid and place the pressure valve to the "Seal" position.
8. Select "Manual" and cook under "High Pressure" for about 25 minutes.
9. Select "Cancel" and carefully do a "Natural" release.
10. Remove the lid and transfer the duck onto a cutting board.
11. Cut into desired sized pieces and serve.

**Nutrition Information per Serving:**

| Calories | Fat | Carbohydrates | Protein |
|---|---|---|---|
| 920 | 69.2 grams | 0.5 grams | 69 grams |

**Roasted Quails**

| Yield | Preparation Time | Cooking Time |
|---|---|---|
| 4 servings | 15 minutes | 23 minutes |

**Ingredients:**

- 2 (5 ounce) whole quails, cleaned and emptied and rinsed
- Salt and freshly ground black pepper, to taste
- 1 fresh thyme bunch
- 1 fresh rosemary bunch
- ½ cup homemade chicken broth
- 3 ½ ounces bacon, chopped
- ½ small yellow onion, chopped finely
- 1/8 teaspoon dried rosemary
- 1/8 teaspoon dried thyme
- 1 bay leaf

**Directions:**

1. Season the quails with salt and black pepper slightly.
2. Stuff the cavity of quails with fresh herb bunches.
3. Place the oil in the Instant Pot and select "Sauté." Then add the bacon, onion, dried herbs, bay leaf, salt, and black pepper and cook for about 3 minutes.
4. Place the quails in the pot, breast side down and cook for about 4-5 minutes or until browned completely.
5. Flip the side and now place the quails breast side up.
6. Select "Cancel" and add the broth into the pot.
7. Secure the lid and place the pressure valve to the "Seal" position.
8. Select "Manual" and cook under "High Pressure" for about 7-9 minutes.
9. Select "Cancel" and carefully do a "Quick" release.
10. Remove the lid and with tongs transfer quails onto a plate.
11. Then remove the herb sprigs from cavity.
12. Strain the liquid into a bowl.
13. Return the broth in the Instant Pot and select "Sauté."
14. Cook for about 3-4 minutes.
15. Add the quail and cook for about 2 minutes, pouring the sauce over the quails occasionally.
16. Remove the lid and serve the quails with the sauce.

**Nutrition Information per Serving:**

| Calories | Fat | Carbohydrates | Protein |
| --- | --- | --- | --- |
| 586 | 31 grams | 2.7 grams | 70 grams |

# Dessert Recipes

**Yogurt Custard**

| Yield | Preparation Time | Cooking Time |
|---|---|---|
| 6 servings | 10 minutes | 20 minutes |

**Ingredients:**

- 1 cup plain Greek yogurt
- 2 cups full-fat coconut milk
- ½ cup Swerve
- 2 teaspoons ground cardamom

**Directions:**

1. Arrange a steamer trivet in the bottom of the Instant Pot and pour in one cup of water.
2. In a heatproof pan, mix together all of the ingredients.
3. With a piece of foil, cover the pan.
4. Place the pan on top of the trivet.
5. Secure the lid and place the pressure valve to the "Seal" position.
6. Select "Manual" and cook under "High Pressure" for about 20 minutes.
7. Select "Cancel" and carefully do a "Natural" release for about 10 minutes, and then do a "Quick" release.
8. Remove the lid and keep aside to cool.
9. Refrigerate to chill before serving.

**Nutrition Information per Serving:**

| Calories | Fat | Carbohydrates | Protein |
|---|---|---|---|
| 216 | 19.6 grams | 7 grams | 4.2 grams |

## Chocolate Mousse

| Yield | Preparation Time | Cooking Time |
|---|---|---|
| 6 servings | 15 minutes | 10 minutes |

### Ingredients:

- 4 organic egg yolks
- ½ cup Swerve
- ¼ cup cacao powder
- ¼ cup water
- 1 cup whipping cream
- ½ cup unsweetened almond milk
- ½ teaspoon vanilla extract
- ¼ teaspoon salt

**Directions:**

1. In a bowl, add the egg yolks and beat well. Set aside.
2. In a pan, add the Swerve, cacao, and water and beat until well combined.
3. Add the cream and almond milk and beat until well combined.
4. Cook until just heated, stirring continuously.
5. Immediately remove from the heat and stir in the vanilla extract and salt. Set aside to cool slightly.
6. Add about one tablespoon of warm chocolate mixture into the bowl of egg yolks and beat until well combined.
7. Slowly add the remaining chocolate mixture, beating continuously until well combined.
8. Transfer the mixture into five ramekins.
9. In the bottom of the Instant Pot, arrange a steamer trivet and pour in 1 ½ cups of water.
10. Place the ramekins on top of the trivet.
11. Secure the lid and place the pressure valve to the "Seal" position.
12. Select "Manual" and cook under "High Pressure" for about 6 minutes.
13. Select "Cancel" and carefully do a "Quick" release.
14. Remove the lid and transfer the ramekins onto a counter to cool completely.
15. Refrigerate to chill before serving.

**Nutrition Information per Serving:**

| Calories | Fat | Carbohydrates | Protein |
|---|---|---|---|
| 129 | 12.2 grams | 3.7 grams | 3.6 grams |

## Crème Brûlée

| Yield | Preparation Time | Cooking Time |
|---|---|---|
| 3 servings | 15 minutes | 6 minutes |

**Ingredients:**

- 7 teaspoons Swerve, divided
- 1 cup heavy cream
- 3 organic egg yolks, beaten
- 1 teaspoon organic vanilla extract

**Directions:**

1. In a large bowl, add five teaspoons of Swerve and remaining ingredients and beat until well combined.
2. Through a fine mesh sieve, strain the mixture into a bowl.
3. Now, place the mixture into three custard cups.
4. With a piece of foil, cover each cup.
5. Arrange a steamer trivet in the bottom of the Instant Pot and pour in 1 ½ cups of water.
6. Place the custard cups on top of the trivet.

7. Secure the lid and place the pressure valve to the "Seal" position.
8. Select "Manual" and cook under "High Pressure" for about 6 minutes.
9. Select "Cancel" and carefully do a "Natural" release for about 10 minutes and then do a "Quick" release.
10. Remove the lid and place the custard cups onto a wire rack.
11. Remove the foil pieces and let them cool.
12. After cooling, cover the cups with plastic wrap and refrigerate overnight.
13. Remove from refrigerator and with a paper towel carefully pat on the crème to remove any moisture.
14. Sprinkle remaining Swerve over each cup evenly.
15. With a culinary torch, melt the Swerve until caramelized.
16. Serve immediately.

**Nutrition Information per Serving:**

| Calories | Fat | Carbohydrates | Protein |
|---|---|---|---|
| 89 | 8.3 grams | 2.8 grams | 1.5 grams |

## Lemon Cheesecake

| Yield | Preparation Time | Cooking Time |
|---|---|---|
| 6 servings | 15 minutes | 30 minutes |

**Ingredients:**

- ¼ cup plus 1 teaspoon Truvia
- 8 ounces cream cheese, softened
- 1/3 cup Ricotta cheese
- 1 teaspoon grated fresh lemon zest
- 2 tablespoons fresh lemon juice
- ½ teaspoon lemon extract
- 2 organic eggs
- 2 tablespoons sour cream

**Directions:**

1. In a bowl, add ¼ cup of Truvia and remaining ingredients except the eggs and sour cream and with a mixer beat on high speed until smooth.
2. Add eggs and beat on low speed until well combined.
3. Transfer the mixture into a six-inch greased spring-form pan evenly.
4. With a piece of foil, cover the pan.
5. In the bottom of the Instant Pot, arrange a steamer trivet and pour in two cups of water.
6. Place the spring-form pan on top of the trivet.
7. Secure the lid and place the pressure valve to the "Seal" position.
8. Select "Manual" and cook under "High Pressure" for about 30 minutes.
9. Select "Cancel" and carefully do a "Natural" release.
10. Remove the lid and transfer the pan onto a wire rack.
11. Set aside to cool slightly.
12. Meanwhile, in a small bowl, add sour cream and remaining Truvia and beat until well combined.
13. Spread cream mixture on the warm cake evenly.
14. Refrigerate for about 6-8 hours before serving.
15. Cut into desired sized slices and serve.

**Nutrition Information per Serving:**

| Calories | Fat | Carbohydrates | Protein |
|---|---|---|---|
| 183 | 16.6 grams | 5.3 grams | 6.5 grams |

## Chocolate Cakes

| Yield | Preparation Time | Cooking Time |
|---|---|---|
| 2 servings | 15 minutes | 9 minutes |

- 2 large organic eggs
- 2 tablespoons Swerve
- 2 tablespoons heavy cream
- ¼ cup cacao powder
- ½ teaspoon organic baking powder

**Directions:**
1. In a bowl, add the eggs, Splenda, and cream and beat until well combined.
2. Add the cacao powder and baking powder and mix until well combined.
3. Place the mixture into two greased ramekins about halfway full.
4. Arrange a steamer trivet in the bottom of the Instant Pot and pour in one cup of water.
5. Place the ramekins on top of the trivet.
6. Secure the lid and place the pressure valve to the "Seal" position.
7. Select "Manual" and cook under "High Pressure" for about 9 minutes.
8. Select "Cancel" and carefully do a "Quick" release.
9. Remove the lid and carefully, flip onto a plate.
10. Serve warm.

| Calories | Fat | Carbohydrates | Protein |
|---|---|---|---|
| 154 | 12.5 grams | 8 grams | 8.6 grams |

Can I ask you for a Quick Favor?

**Would you, please, leave this book review on Amazon?**

Reviews are very important for me as they help me to sell more books and to understand how to move forward. This will enable me to write more books.

Thank you for reading so much!

Want more?

Here it is!

**Get 2 weeks meal plan and shopping list for this cookbook**

https://ellenbranson.wixsite.com/mysite

Just visit the link above to download it

I am sure you will love it!

Thank you!

Ellen Branson.

**Other books by Ellen:**

Made in United States
Cleveland, OH
18 February 2025